MW00466542

The Chosen Ones

An Addicts Guide To Their True Purpose

by

Dr. Nicole Ouzounian

DORRANCE
PUBLISHING CO
EST. 1920
PITTSBURGH, PENNSYLVANIA 15238

The contents of this work, including, but not limited to, the accuracy of events, people, and places depicted; opinions expressed; permission to use previously published materials included; and any advice given or actions advocated are solely the responsibility of the author, who assumes all liability for said work and indemnifies the publisher against any claims stemming from publication of the work.

All Rights Reserved
Copyright © 2021 by Dr. Nicole Ouzounian

No part of this book may be reproduced or transmitted, downloaded, distributed, reverse engineered, or stored in or introduced into any information storage and retrieval system, in any form or by any means, including photocopying and recording, whether electronic or mechanical, now known or hereinafter invented without permission in writing from the publisher.

Dorrance Publishing Co
585 Alpha Drive
Pittsburgh, PA 15238
Visit our website at *www.dorrancebookstore.com*

ISBN: 978-1-6366-1182-2
eISBN: 978-1-6366-1772-5

I dedicate this book to all of the addicts struggling with drug and/ or alcohol addiction. There is not a day that goes by that I am not inspired by those who I am blessed to work for. Watching individuals fight for their lives, giving everything they have to transform their souls is a powerful reminder of just how strong we can truly be. I have great respect and admiration for those struggling with addiction and am honored to be fighting the fight with you.

Table of Contents

The Chosen Ones

Chapter 1:

The Destructive Path of Addiction and the Blessings of Recovery

✠ IT IS IMPOSSIBLE TO PUT INTO WORDS the ritualistic practices and all out efforts required to maintain a prescription addiction. Non-addicts will provide endless words of judgmental advice believing it's as simple as putting the drugs down. We've been hearing in the news how Opioid addiction has reached epidemic proportions in the United States. If it were that easy to put the pills down, don't you think the billions of people addicted would do just that!?

In 2001, Winona Ryder was charged with shoplifting and a prescription of narcotics were found in her possession. In 2003, Rush Limbaugh, sixty-six-years-old, announced that he was addicted to Oxycontin and checked himself into a treatment center in Palm Beach County, Florida. Cindy McCain, wife of late Republican Politician Senator Jim McCain, developed an addiction to Oxycontin after she was prescribed the medication to alleviate pain following two spinal surgeries and to ease emotional stress. The above mentioned are the lucky ones who have not yet allowed this disease to completely destroy them.

Actor Heath Ledger died of a drug overdose in 2008 at twenty-nine-years-old. Oxycodone was found in in his system. Actor Cory Monteith from the show *Glee*, died at twenty-three from an accidental overdose of heroin and alcohol in 2013. In 2014, actor Philip Seymour Hoffman, age forty-six, died of acute intoxication by heroin, cocaine, amphetamine, and benzodiazepine use. Singer and songwriter Prince died of an accidental fentanyl overdose in 2016 and joined the growing list of entertainers not exempt from this disease.

The people mentioned above didn't start out as addicts and regretfully most probably had no idea where their addiction was taking them. At one time, they were idealistic artists ready to take on the world, only to be transformed to a shell of themselves, wondering, "Where did I go?" I've had the awesome pleasure of working with hundreds, if not thousands, of people throughout my career whose addictions mirror that of the high-profile lucky individuals mentioned above. Sadly, I have also lost many clients to this insidious problem. What I found in my almost two decades of work is that many people addicted to prescription pills, illicit drugs, and/ or alcohol are amazing individuals who grew up in loving homes, received an education, had a great deal of compassion, empathy, and sensitivity, while gifted with some form of incredible talent. These beautiful qualities do not disappear when pills are brought into the picture, but they do get repressed, held within the confines of some internal energy closet if you will, until ready to emerge again, in a healthy, more productive, and polished way. The process is knowing the self, losing the self, and finding a new self. I am happy to say that many people I have worked with have emerged victorious from this difficult to understand phenomenon. Below are three example profiles of actual clients I have had the honor of working with. Their names are changed to ensure confidentiality.

Christy

Christy is a thirty-five-year-old, Caucasian, female attorney who lives in Fort Lauderdale, Florida. She has been married for three years to her husband, whom she met five years ago online. Her husband is a professor at the local university and teaches biology. They have no children. She has been working with the same law firm for the past ten years, the job she obtained immediately after passing her bar exam when she was twenty-five.

Christy always liked to party since she was a teenager, and when she went to college, she was placed on academic probation due to her grades falling and not attending classes. Her parents were very concerned at the time due to her paternal uncle passing away of cirrhosis of the liver. They convinced Christy to go into therapy, and she was able to complete college as well as law school, binge drinking frequently, unable to obtain total abstinence. The binge drinking never stopped, and Christy continued to binge drink about once per month against her husband's and family's desires for her to stop. The consequences of Christy's drinking hadn't hit levels of severe concern at this point because Christy was able to manage most of her life the other twenty-nine days of the month.

About two years ago, Christy had to have surgery on her shoulder and was prescribed Percocet. She began taking the medication as prescribed but liked the way it numbed her physically as well as emotionally. She began drinking more frequently while she would take the pills and had to go to her doctor before her prescription was due for a refill because she was taking more than what was prescribed. She convinced her doctor to fill a new prescription and quickly escalated to taking ten to fifteen pills per day along with drinking three to four drinks per day. Throughout this time, she was hiding her use from her husband and her parents. When she went back to her doctor in an attempt to get her prescription filled again, her doctor refused. This is when Christy began Dr. shopping. For about one year, Christy went from doctor to doctor with her use progressing from Percocet to Vicodin to OxyContin, ingesting about fifteen pills per day. In addition, her alcohol use increased from binge drinking one time per month to drinking four to five drinks per day.

About one year ago Christy's husband found out about the pill and alcohol use and confronted her along with Christy's parents. Christy promised she would stop and truly attempted to, but on the first day she woke up and felt very high levels of anxiety, stomach pains, body aches, was shaking, had restless legs, and had severe flu like symptoms. Her body was craving the pills, so she immediately and secretly started using again. Her husband found out when he started noticing some of their belongings were missing as well as money from their savings account. He noticed that she was not going to work the way that she used to and used the excuse that she is now allowed to work from home 80 percent of the time. It became normal for him to find Christy passed out on the couch or in their bed when he would come home from work. He ended up learning that she was lying about her job, and she was actually terminated from her job as a result of too many unexcused absences and no call and no shows. He confronted her and basically told her that if she doesn't get the help she needs, he is going to leave her. Christy already lost her job, she was ignoring her parents because she did not want them to know how bad her addiction had gotten, and she was about to lose her husband and her home, and she could feel that her health was deteriorating. She made a very important phone call after coming clean to her parents and her husband about the severity of her use and her fears about her health and sanity. With the support of her husband and parents, Christy was admitted into a detox center.

Unfortunately, Christy's story is not that uncommon. We are living in a time that allows one to be susceptible to all kinds of addictions. With the internet and social media technologies leading the way in creating a culture that perpetuates an instant gratification mentality, it should come as no surprise that many Americans are choosing quick fixes to alleviate physical pain, mental pain, and/ or social dysfunctions. We have become trained and programed to think this way. Leading the way in this modern mindset is the field of medicine. If there is something ailing you, there is a prescription medication that will provide instant relief. Sadly, the cost of abusing prescription medications does not always outweigh the benefits, and many of our nation's people are struggling with the intense consequences of living a life that includes medications originally designed to give one comfort from intense chronic pain, like Christy.

Cody

Cody was another client of mine who was unaware of the intense addictive potentials of prescription pain medications. Cody was a twenty-seven-year-old male when I began working with him whose drug of choice ended up progressing to heroin. He reported that his addiction started when he was twenty-years-old after being prescribed opiates due to a dirt bike accident. He shared that five years later, he began injecting heroin because he couldn't afford paying for the amount of prescriptions required to deliver the effects he wanted from the substance. The stigma of addiction almost deterred Cody from receiving help and fears of what his family would think kept him quiet, holding this secret for years.

His addiction had gotten so bad that he finally admitted to his family he was physically and mentally dependent on heroin. He had to acknowledge he was behaving in ways that just weren't him. He was stealing from his parents and from his employer but was so detached from his behaviors because his only role in life was to get high and stay high. Even during this time, he would say to himself, "I'm not a criminal" and would justify how he would pay everyone back he stole from. He shared with me, "I didn't know who I was anymore."

He shared about the guilt and shame he put on his family due to his addiction. He admitted to not knowing how to have relationships and feeling sorry for himself, blaming doctors for his addiction. This victim mentality is what kept him sick during his active addiction. Awareness allowed him to take responsibility for his recovery. Cody shared that the biggest change he has seen within himself as a result of his transformational experience is the way he thinks. He shared that while in his active addiction he was "ego driven" and "self-centered." He shared that he now has "self-awareness" and has "self-worth," utilizing everything he learned from the experience to help other people struggling with addictions.

Jake

Jake, a thirty-six-year-old male whose drug of choice was Vicodin, shared that his addiction started when he was twenty-five after being prescribed Vicodin for a concussion. He admitted to immediately liking the way Vicodin made him feel and quickly began abusing it. Once his body became addicted to the substance, he believed he had no control over its use, and the power of choice was removed. He confessed that everything addiction related became a priority, whether it was the lifestyle or the using of the substance itself. He couldn't believe how this boy who grew up in a suburban, middle class Connecticut home, with loving parents, began stealing, lying, and manipulating for selfish gains to feed his addiction. Where did this boy and vibrant young man go? He shared how he would go to work "high" and actually begin to withdraw, leaving his office early many days because of the intense pain of withdrawal, needing to take more Vicodin to stop the pain. He shared how he lost his friends, ignored his family, and had to go on leave from his high-profile law firm because Vicodin was his everything, and he didn't care.

He shared how crazy his life was because nothing mattered but, at the same time, everything mattered. He wanted to stop using desperately but didn't know how. The hardest part for Jake was to accept he had a problem because he always appeared to be in control. Once this awareness occurred, he was ready and actually wanting to do what was required to transform his soul. He had a strong belief that an addicted person had to commit and actually commit daily to their recovery. He explained, "it takes a commitment, a daily commitment to do whatever it is that is required to get roots in your sobriety."

Jake has been sober for three years and has since changed professions, working in the field of addiction in Florida, helping struggling addicts find the help they need. He has a positive relationships with his family and believes he is now a productive member of society helping to change the world one person at a time.

From Addiction to Recovery

The enigmatic power of prescription pills has no words as it has the potential of becoming one's god. The levels of consequences all three clients were willing to endure to continue to serve this prescription god is something only an addict would understand. The rationalizations and justifications which occur to maintain the lifestyle are quite genius. The levels of darkness that must be tapped into to maintain the addiction are beyond most people's levels of understanding, and the strongholds which keep people sick and suffering appear to be beyond this world. Most of the clients I have worked with have said things like, "I wasn't me in my addiction," using words like "I felt possessed." All clients have said how they did things in their addiction they would have never ever done sober. All said they lost themselves and didn't know where they went!

All three individuals mentioned above are presently working in the addiction field in some capacity and are now extraordinary present-day miracles, guiding others to find their own miracles. All three individuals were on a path to destruction, living in their own personal hells, but they found another way and they chose to follow this new way. They found a new and improved way, an enlightened way of being of which they would have never discovered had they not went down the road of addiction. Chapter 2 will discuss how my dark path led me to the light.

Chapter 2:

A Recruiter is Born

W<small>HAT</small> I <small>AM ABOUT TO WRITE MAY BE</small> relatable to some and completely crazy to others. A little bit of background before we get into the truth about addiction and how the dark uses it to recruit. My name is Nicole Ouzounian, and I have been on a quest to figure out this thing called life since I was five; yes, five years old. It was then when I looked in the mirror, and I asked God to teach me whatever I had to learn so I could become what He wanted me to become. It was around this time that I started noticing something was a bit off with me. What does this mean? Well, I could feel people. Not feel them in a sense where I would touch them and feel them, but I could feel people. I could feel when they were angry, sad, happy, anxious, nervous, fatigued, energetic, hopeful, hopeless, etc. I guess you could say I was blessed or cursed, depending on how one looks at it, with the ability to feel other people's energy. Yes, it began at five, and now at forty-six, many (but not all) of my questions have been answered as to why I have been blessed with this empathic gift.

Looking back, there were so many nightmares and prophetic dreams preparing me for what God wanted me to do. I was about six-years-old when my family and I moved to Arizona. I remember living in a small yellow and green house. This is when my nightmares started. For some reason I was always afraid to sleep by myself. I had this crazy fear that I would see a ghost, or some monster was going to come and get me. One night I was trying to fall asleep, and when I opened my eyes, I could have sworn I saw a black shadow running in the hallway. Could this have been one of the shadow people or the dark human like figures hiding in the corner that can only be seen with our peripheral vision (You know what I mean crystal meth addicts)? I screamed in terror. My dad came running into my room, and I told him what I saw. He thought I had an overactive imagination and sat with me for a while until I fell asleep. I have never forgotten this vision.

There were many nights I would have nightmares or felt there were other spirits in my room besides myself. One night I was sleeping and woke up instantly. To this day, I remember it like it was yesterday. I could have sworn I saw big beautiful cats circling my bed. Leopards, jaguars, black panthers, and tigers; what was going on? At the time, I didn't think they were beautiful. I thought they were going to eat me. This was my first experience with animal spirits. When I think about it now, I know they were protecting me. It's as if the divine had to protect me from the dark forces until I was old enough to learn how to protect myself.

After about four-years of living in Arizona, my parents decided to call it quits. They just weren't getting along. I'm really not sure if they ever really did. The arguments would be so intense at times, my brother and I would yell from our rooms, "Be Quiet," because we couldn't sleep. I will never forget when I was about seven, overhearing my parents talking from their hiding place in the bathroom about getting a divorce. Their hiding place wasn't a good one. I heard everything and cried for hours.

My brother, mother, and I moved into a three-bedroom apartment on the border of Phoenix and Scottsdale. I realize now that the universe had been exposing me to things we cannot see with our human eyes for years. This apartment exposed me to even more, and there is not a doubt in my mind that it was definitely haunted. I would hear footsteps at night in the living room. This would happen every night. It would be like the sound you hear when someone is walking loudly on carpet. This is the only way I can explain it. It wasn't the best neighborhood either, so the creepy feelings in the apartment as well as outside the apartment made it scary at night. My brother and I would take turns sleeping with my mom in her room because I think we were all a bit uncomfortable.

One night it was my brother's turn to sleep with my mom, and I went to my own room. I heard a bang in the bathroom next to me and ran upstairs telling my mom and brother what I heard. My mom told me to turn the bathroom light on, and I would be fine. So I calmed down, turned the bathroom light on, and crawled into bed. Within five minutes, the bathroom light turned off on its own. I screamed bloody murder! I don't think I have ever screamed so loud and for so long ever in my life. My mother and brother came running into my room. I think I scared them more than the ghost scared me. The spirits definitely wanted me to know they were there.

Questions began to enter my mind? Did other people have experiences like this? Did they feel people? Did they have dreams and visions of animals and shadow people? It's really not something one talks about openly. What's a girl to do? I repressed everything! I didn't talk about anything weird and I tried to blend in with the crowd, or the herd if you will.

It was around sixteen-years-old when I began partying. Alcohol and weed became my weekend friends. I actually felt like I blended in with my peers when I was drinking and drugging. I finally felt like I was connecting to people, and my social anxieties of being a weirdo were gone! But there were consequences of trying to fit in this way that I was not yet aware of. I'm not going to get into my years of pill use and addiction but what needs to be mentioned; when I was using, I had minimal access to the light. It was almost as if the dark was closer, pulling me into its dimension. At that point it didn't matter, I was hanging out with people and I finally felt like I belonged. The consequences didn't matter at that point because the sense of belonging was too powerful.

I had always been sensitive to energies, dark or light, it made no difference. The darker I became, the more I used alcohol and drugs. This is when everything turned. What once helped me feel connected to others, now was having the opposite effect moving from a place of hope to feeling hopeless.

Fast forward a few more years. I was high on Adderall and vodka. My mood was beyond anger. I hated myself, I hated the man I was with at the time, and I hated life in general. I laid down to try and sleep when all of the sudden the horrible smell of sulfur was all around me. I didn't know what it was, so I walked around the apartment I was living in at the time looking for the source of the smell. After about two minutes of me looking for where the smell was coming from, I saw it. I saw a mirage, shadow, apparition if you will. It was pure evil. I was petrified and knew it was a demon. It wanted me, but I was not ready to surrender to its dark temptations. I immediately dropped to my knees and prayed for the blood of Jesus Christ to protect me. It was gone! What I realized soon after was I was the cause of the demon entering my home due to my negative dark attitude and behaviors. This was not my first experience with a demon, but it was the first time that I invited it into my home. I had become so intimate with the dark that it wanted me even closer and entered my realm, my home, and my reality. This was when I learned just how powerful our emotions in relation to the power of attraction and manifestation really are.

Even after seeing an actual demon and smelling the horrible sent of putrid sulfur, I was not done. The following weekend, I drank and took some prescription pills prescribed to reduce my anxiety, and I became horribly depressed. It was a depression I had never felt before. The feeling was so incredibly hopeless and dark, I wanted to leave this earth. Even as I write these words, tears are streaming down my face as to what I almost did! I decided that night was going to be the night I ended my life. I had thoughts of wanting to commit suicide in the past but never as strong as I did that night. It was as if something continuously was whispering in my ear, "You can end the pain, Nicole." The voice was loud, encouraging, and even motivating. I took many pills and drank an enormous amount of alcohol, hoping I would not wake up. The demon taunting me was not going to make this easy, but neither was God! Within thirty minutes, I was having incredible stomach pains. Could I not even die in peace? Something snapped, and I realized, what the heck did I just do? I immediately called 911, told them what I had done, and I was involuntarily committed to a psychiatric hospital. This was the worst day of my life but was a very necessary part of my journey. This experience was the catalyst that brought me out of the dark and introduced me to my purpose.

Stories upon stories of unexplainable occurrences. I could go on for pages and pages, but I won't. I believe we are all trained for whatever purpose God has for us. Every moment prepares us for the next moment. That being said, I believe that there are some people born in this realm that have been gifted with the opportunity to see things that other people do not with the purpose of maintaining the balance of the Universe. One of the gifts, yes I said gifts, of addiction is that it allows one to be intimate with that which we cannot see. It opens portals to other dimensions, providing information of expanded Universal truths. The caveat, in order to become intimate with the light, I believe one has to have been intimate with the dark. The challenge: can one let go of the dark and its lifestyle and fully submit to the light and its lifestyle?

In retrospect, based on my spiritual, personal, and professional experiences, I consider myself to be a recruiter for God, an ambassador if you will. My target population is addicts as I believe this is who God wants me to minister to. Throughout my career, the majority of my clients have reported heroin or opiates as their drug of choice, but alcohol, Xanax, crystal meth, and cocaine are usually in the mix. There is no defined demographic I could disclose explaining what an addict looks like. Everyone is susceptible and many begin with doctor prescribed medications that quickly escalate from use, to abuse, to dependence, and finally to an addiction.

I believe I was called into the addiction field by my higher power. Working in the field of addiction has enlightened me to the true strength of the human spirit. I have witnessed and helped individuals transform from despair to discovering the strength and wisdom within themselves. The people I train have seen and experienced things beyond their level of understanding. The people I train have already had experiences utilizing a higher power to accomplish incredible feats. They connect to a source greater than themselves, which provides internal and external resources to sustain their addictive lifestyle. Please don't misunderstand, the higher power of which I am speaking of is the power of the dark, not the light. Addicts have already tapped into universal energies, which provides them strength to continue a very difficult and expensive lifestyle with minimal resources. This lifestyle would not be maintained for a consistent period of time if addicted individuals did not tap into something bigger than themselves that could restore them to insanity (we will discuss this in depth later)! You cannot have one without the other. If there is God, there must be Satan. I have not met one addict who has not been introduced to the dark. If there is dark then there must be light. An individual addicted to drugs and/or alcohol has no choice, they must choose a side, or the side will choose them! The beautiful part of all this is that the universe is always working with us. Chapter 3 explains some of the ways the universe speaks to us. Are you listening?

Chapter 3:
A Solution

SUCH AN EXCESSIVE AND PERSISTENT PERSON I AM. There were so many things I wanted for myself when I was trying to figure out what all the pain was for. I wanted to be happy, I wanted to feel peaceful, I wanted to be able to enjoy all areas of my life while having the ability to flow with life and not fight it. I knew it was somewhere inside me, I just didn't know how to tap into it.

I do have to admit, I tried to take the easy way to enlightenment. I always fought the fact that I needed to change me. So I would read books, pray, and dream about how I wanted to be, but I never changed me. I was always angry at people, my family, my ex-husband, my so-called friends, myself, the weather – you name it, I was angry at it! I expected people to have more patience, my ex-husband to love me the way I wanted to be loved, my family to nurture and support any decision that I made, and my friends to never stab me in the back or lie to me. I expected to make better choices, and I expected beautiful weather, especially when I had to drive in it. I thought because I read all of these spiritual books and understood what they said, I should automatically be at peace. I can honestly say, and I 100 percent know, there is no easy way! There is no way of cutting corners, and I needed to experience life and transform within to find true peace.

After years and years of trying to figure myself out I finally learned, stop looking outside of yourself for answers. This had gotten me nowhere. There came a time when I had to convince myself, it was time to truly go inside. No more excuses of using external situations, people, employers, colleagues, peers, family, and personal appearance to distract me while dictating my negative attitudes creating a life of which I thought I needed something outside of myself, like a mind-altering substance, to make me feel better! Letting go of something I loved and hated so much felt like something had died in me. Maybe this was a good thing. Something must die in order to be reborn. It is amazing how many times I have been reborn!

> PROVERBS 20:5 *The purposes of the human mind are like deep water, but the intelligent will draw them out.*

Let us take a closer look at the insanity of it all. We ask our higher power to help us but then we poo poo the help we receive. The crazy part is that we cannot move forward until we learn the lessons of today.

How do you learn a lesson?

The problem with learning a lesson is that if you do not learn it, it will come back to bite you in the butt over and over and over again. Seeing as how one of the main qualities of an addict is that we are stubborn, addicts seem to get bit quite a bit. Or I should speak about myself. I swear, I am learning lessons that started when I was five. We must remember that transformation is a process that requires time, effort, and that lovely virtue we all so desperately lack, patience.

> PROVERBS 19:19 *A violent person will pay the penalty; if you effect a rescue, you will only have to do it again.*

I read this verse and was like wow, I totally agree. You see, the "violent" could be any character flaw (i.e. addiction, anger, isolation, fear, lack of patience, pride, etc.). The rescue, I believe, are signs, symbols and help we receive, whether from the divine or from people, to change these character flaws in order to refine ourselves, embrace our gifts, and create a life filled with love that doesn't include pills. If we don't change the flaws that are screaming to be changed, we will only suffer as a result of hanging onto them.

Talk about stubborn. If God were to give me anymore signs, there would be no more reasons for faith to exist (we all know faith is believing in something we cannot see), because he nearly showed himself to me many times literally saying, what is wrong with you? It is amazing how a sign could be so powerful one minute and have such little significance the next. I began to learn how embracing the signs allowed me to tap into the secrets of getting what I wanted while being addiction free. We must never forget; this is about progress not perfection!

So, one of my lessons that needed to be learned was, I had to stop thinking I knew what was best for me. I would hang on for dear life to whatever this thing was. Whether it was a pill, a thought, an attitude, alcohol or whatever, I wouldn't let it go because I thought I needed it. I would receive signs that told me the path I was heading down was taking me into a very dark dimension. I was being told "*stop*" because there was a better way. So I knew this intellectually, but I didn't trust it in my soul. As a result, I continued going the direction I knew was wrong and would become upset when things turned out poorly. It sounds so crazy because even after ignoring all the signs and continuing my dark behaviors, I would say to myself, "Why is this happening to me? What did I do to deserve this?" I would torture myself by hanging on to old thoughts and behaviors instead of releasing and letting go. Sounds so easy to just release and let go! Well, I guess it might be if we would learn how to do it and trust that we could. I thought all I needed to do was love God and I would be okay. I learned the hard way the secret to a great life is to not only love God, but it is quit necessary to follow his will because the human will is all about human desire.

The wacky thing about lessons is that we ask for them; or, at least I believe we do. God, please help me be more patient. God, please make me mentally stronger. God, please take the desire for the pills away. It would be really great if when we asked for something, it just happened, but we all know it's not that easy.

So why does nothing change? Why do people continue with old behaviors they want to let go of? Why do they still suffer, lie, hide, manipulate and keep secrets. Why is it the more we ask for God to help us the worse things get? *Ah ha!* Could this be the answer? Would a person change a situation if the consequences weren't life changing? There is really no other way to break the unexplainable body, mind, and soul attachments that come with addiction unless the circumstances become so detrimental that the individual suffering can no longer withstand the internal and external conflicts associated with the behaviors. You see, problems increase because the Universe is screaming at us to make life altering adjustments. We must learn to understand how the universe speaks to us and spiritually listen for our answered requests and questions it so beautifully reveals. If we don't change how we approach our lessons, we will not learn the lessons that will bring us success in all areas of our lives.

Surprisingly, the world will present situations that teach us the very things we are asking to be taught. Many of us ask to be more patient, more assertive, less co-dependent, more confident, more independent, more positive, more tolerant, and healthier physically and mentally, free from the prescription pills which no longer serve our new purpose. For example, if someone asks to be more patient, their life will be filled with situations where they will need patience, and if they are still not exhibiting the quality of patience, they will continue to be presented with circumstances that will require patience. If someone is asking to be free from addiction, the universe will provide resources to do so. It will happen again and again and again. If you do not take the help the universe so lovingly provides, you will continue to suffer in ways that will create severe strife and contention within your life and within the lives of those you love. The factors that create the strife and contention may not present in the exact same ways, but the experiences will be similar. It may present in a different venue or place with different actors or people, or it may be the same venue or place, with the same actors or people. For example, I left an alcoholic boyfriend only to begin a new relationship with another addict because I didn't learn the lesson. Things got so bad with this boyfriend, I then left him, but only to get into another relationship with a man that had more of an addiction. I was asking the universe to help me become an independent strong woman and yet I was settling in all my relationships, miserable in every single one of them not learning the lesson.

Changing our external world will require we look within our own world. By changing ourselves, we will transform unhealthy connections with people we so dearly love while having the ability to reconnect with family and friends. Again, if we don't change how we approach our lessons, we will not learn the lessons to have success in all areas of our lives. If nothing changes, nothing changes.

Staying humble in your growth is necessary to maintain the growth. The thing about learning lessons and obtaining knowledge and wisdom is that something could always come back and show you, you have not mastered this game called life. Ten steps forward twenty steps back! The universe will continue to shake up your path because the external world doesn't change. You can only change the inside of yourself. Crap outside of you will always be there. The good news, the crap inside of you can be cleaned up. Never, ever get cocky with what you know, who you know, or where you think you are in this classroom called life!

You must be the change you wish to see in the world

— Mahatma Gandhi

Closing a Door Opens a Window

I have pretty incredible dreams at times. One night many years ago when I was still struggling with my own addiction I had what I call a prophetic dream. I was in a world that didn't feel too good. Samson (my cat at the time) was with me. There were two dogs, both of them Saint Bernards, one of them bigger than the other. They kind of directed me towards a nasty house. This house had dirt all around it. Boy was it dirty! I needed to crawl through a window to get out of this house/world. I didn't fit through the opening. Samson jumped right through it. I realized very quickly that all I had to do was open the window wider. I did and went through. I wasn't out of the fog yet. I ended up in this dude's house who was partying with a few people. He asked me if I wanted to join them and go to a place called the "Black Bar." I said no, so Samson and I proceeded to walk away, and then I woke up.

We've all heard the saying, when one door closes, a window or another door opens. Unfortunately, we have to close one door and we really have no idea what's behind the other door or window. Closing a door means we have to let go of old belief systems that keep us sick, imprisoned in our mental cells. These belief systems include what we think of ourselves, what we think of others, and what we think of our world. The ability to open one's mind to possibilities of what could be requires an open-minded student, ready to begin the training required to unlearn things that were once learned. This includes changing a negatively perceived identity to an identity filled with confidence, courage, and limitless possibilities.

The stigma attached to addiction has forever been negative as society has not completely accepted the fact that it is not a moral issue and has a difficult time understanding that it is much bigger than people think on a human and spiritual level. Treatment centers utilize many unsuccessful techniques in an attempt to treat something way beyond most people's levels of understanding. Providing addictive prescription medications to get people off of prescription pills seems very counter intuitive, and as you will see in the next chapter, has never worked, only increasing the suffering and addictive potentials for people who utilize this form of care.

We must be careful what we utilize to heal our emotional and spiritual wounds so our God given gifts can be utilized in the way the light intended them to be used. Closing a door makes people susceptible so it will take incredible strength from within and incredible people around you to not just agree to certain addictive techniques for the means of instant gratification. Wasn't instant gratification an enabler for people to immerse themselves into their addictions in the first place? We do not substitute one quick fix with another! Many different windows and doors will be presented, some will move you closer to the light, and others will be strategically placed to move you more into the dark. You must choose wisely!

Chapter 3 focuses on ways the universe speaks to us and how our challenges are training methods intended to help us grow. The next chapter of this book delves into the history of addiction and how cultural stigmas have marginalized the addicted population. Changing these stigmas and empowering ourselves through awareness are much needed steps for transformation to occur. The next few chapters will describe how we become who we become and how we can alter our identity. It will further explain the spiritual war and the important role addicted individuals have within it!

Chapter 4:

It is Not a Moral Issue!

In many instances, it appears that the drug and alcohol field has only recently begun to understand the predisposing factors that increases the chances of becoming an addict and what keeps individuals stuck in this toxic lifestyle. With the incredibly fast shift in the pharmacology world, the demographic of what constitutes a drug addict is no longer what one would expect. There is no discrimination, racism, or favorites when it comes to who is an addict. Anyone, and I mean anyone is susceptible.

History of the Evolution of Addiction and its Stigma in the United States

Addiction treatment in the United States began in the mid-19th century as a result of changes in alcohol and drug consumption and the professionalization of American medicine.Dr. Benjamin Rush, known as the father of addiction medicine, combined his beliefs on science, morality, and colonial psychology, and his many ideas dominated medical thinking for nearly 100 years. During a time when the nation was celebrating its freedom, Rush noticed the levels of intoxication the American soldiers were displaying and believed a nation addicted would never be free. This is not only true for a nation, but also true for the individuals suffering with the corruption. One of his initial treatment recommendations was that opium replace alcohol as a medicine. He believed that opium caused less deterioration and was less addictive. Little did we know this would cause more harm than good!

This radical idea of treating one addiction with another is still used today, and from my experience is unethical and creating an even larger problem. Medications like methadone, Subutex, and suboxone are medications used to treat heroin and other opiate addictions and appear to be more addicting then heroin ever was. Millions of tax federal dollars are used to battle the opioid epidemic, but most of the money is used to research new and improved pharmaceuticals to treat the addiction. Not only that, they are being marketed as a successful and safe way to treat heroin addiction. Have we not learned anything from history?

I am not going to be shy with my opinion. I have met one person in my professional career who said they had a successful experience using suboxone. So why then were they in treatment for opiate dependence? Why were their withdrawals so severe they could barely complete the day's training classes? There were many times we had to send clients on these medications back to the hospital due to severe post-acute withdrawal symptoms. I do not agree with medically managed opiate treatment. If we know history repeats itself and insanity is doing the same thing over and over again and expecting a different result, why do we continue following this insane cycle? We need to stop believing that anything outside of ourselves will bring lasting happiness.

Sorry, I digress. Back to our history lesson.

Initially, Dr. Rush and his colleagues introduced the notion of addiction and the concept of it being a disease, but people of that time were not ready for this modern medical way of thinking due to the negative stigma surrounding addiction. In the book, *Slaying the Dragon* by William White, the history of how drug and alcohol use was treated is explicitly described. It explains the progression of the naiveté of early professionals who believed they had the answers to treat the disorder, but only manifested more negative intrapersonal and interpersonal issues. Access to hospital beds were restricted to individuals who were perceived as worthy and admission was usually denied to those suffering from alcoholism and drug addiction. In addition, White explains in his book that the medical care for people struggling with addiction included interventions like sedation, utilizing instruments to enforce bleeding, electricity machines, and restraining devices. The high levels of stigma attached to individuals suffering with addiction led to harmful medical interventions, and the abhorrent means of medical treatment was the answer to what the medical field did not understand.

Once the medical field began recognizing that the above medical interventions were not working, the emergence of asylum treatment modalities was created in an attempt to keep addicted individuals off the streets and separate from the rest of the communities. Access to medical hospitals continued to be denied by those they believed to be morally unworthy, which were those individuals considered to be addicts. With evolving approaches emerging in the 1900s, some social groups began recognizing the idea that drug and alcohol addiction may not be a moral issue but may be a disease that manifests as a result of biology, psychology, and sociology, an idea that began years ago with Dr. Benjamin Rush.

In the late 1880s, cocaine was recommended for almost all medical issues. In 1889 Dr. W.H. Bentley advocated the use of cocaine for the treatment of morphine addiction believing that cocaine was the premier remedy for the morphine habit that was so prevalent at the time. By the early 1900s, the stigma for opiate addiction became so bad that those addicted would hide their addiction and attempt to stop in secret in their own homes. Medical care was not an option and exposing their addictions was more painful than the pain experienced from acute withdrawal. Seizures, strokes, and death were not uncommon and appeared less of a consequence than exposure.

By 1914, the Harrison Anti-Narcotic Act was passed, which many consider to be the beginning of the war on drugs. The purpose of this act was to force taxes on the sale and distribution of cocoa leaves, opium, and any form of products derived by these products. The act allowed the narcotic to be prescribed for medicinal purposes but not to treat addiction. As a result of this new federal law, physicians who continued to supply narcotics to large numbers of addicted patients were being arrested. Physicians of the US Public Health Service continued to deny responsibility for this particular population, but something had to be done. According to White, Morphine Maintenance Clinics began opening but were closed by 1925, creating a thriving illicit drug market, as they increased the prices of narcotics by as much as 50 percent. Throughout this time physicians remained quiet as it was known how their part played a role in the development of this problem due to their intemperate management of narcotics.

There is an overwhelming number of people using opioids, some for medicinal purposes, some for recreational, and many for both. These pills are in many American homes, placed in medicine cabinets or bedside tables, allowing easy access for children and/ or young adults. Where at one time drinking beer and smoking a "joint" was considered bad behavior at high school parties, our young generation has evolved to crushing oxycodone pills and snorting them intranasally, possibly accessing them from their parents' medicine cabinets or being prescribed the medication themselves due to sports injuries and the like.

It was only a few years ago that pill mills were popping up all over the nation taking advantage of the ever-increasing number of people's whose tolerance to narcotics was increasing, knowing that the legal prescriptions were not going to be enough to sustain the dependence. These doctors (or witch doctors working for the dark) were prescribing anything and everything for anyone who had the income to pay if the price was right. These dark workers were prescribing medications to people who were so sick and suffering, encouraging more drug use and darkness to enter their patients' lives. As a result, many pill addicts had to revert to illicit street drugs because they could no longer pay for the high-priced pill mill process.

Over the past couple years, federal and state authorities have shut down many illegal pharmaceutical distributions, but money is one of the main roots of all evil, and this industry is not going to stop anytime soon due to the multi-billion dollars made from the people who are addicted to their products. Even knowing this, many people in this country are still in denial of this pandemic and how it is affecting every single human being on this planet.

Unfortunately, the negative stigma attached to addiction is still alive. The growing number of individuals who are falling prey to this colossal outbreak is growing daily. The societal stigmas create a concept that to be an addict means you are not worthy, regardless of how the powers that be are creating this reality. This societal idea becomes a part of an addict's individual schema, which only decreases transformational potentials.

With the prohibition of alcohol in the 1920s and the depression in the 1930s, it was a time of great reform. Most institutions designed to treat addiction were gone and the escalation of alcohol and drug addiction could not be ignored. In the 1930s, the Oxford Group, a Christian organization led by Frank Buchman emerged, holding house parties at various locations around the world intended to help alcoholics only. These meetings were not intended for drug addicts because drug addicts were stigmatized by the alcoholics. The Oxford Group was guided by four standards and five procedures. The four standards include honesty, unselfishness, purity, and love. The five procedures for this group were give into God, listen to God's direction, check guidance, restitution, and sharing. This was the beginning of a program that understood addiction was not a moral issue, but actually involved so much more.

A man by the name of Bill Wilson, struggling with alcoholism attended an Oxford Group meeting, getting his first experience of the power of fellowship and the importance of one alcoholic helping another. Wilson soon discovered that he could not stop drinking on his own and he needed others in the fellowship to maintain his sobriety. In 1935, Bill Wilson and a man named Dr. Bob collaborated and created what is today known as Alcoholics Anonymous (AA). This twelve-step model focuses on intrapersonal issues as well as interpersonal connections and ascribes to the idea that following the twelve steps will change the active addict to one who is in recovery. It is probably the most well-known approach in this country designed to move addicts from active addiction to recovery. It believes that addiction is not a moral issue like many medical and behavioral professionals historically believed.

Alcoholics Anonymous meetings are designed to be, you guessed it, anonymous. To have a place to fellowship with other individuals struggling with similar issues, it is aimed at guiding an individual from the dark dimensions into the light dimensions utilizing twelve-steps. But unfortunately, it has a low success rate of recovery because people do not understand that they aren't just steps, they are a roadmap meant to lead people into an entirely new way of life.

Originally meant for alcoholics only, AA now allows all suffering addicts to attend their meetings, join their fellowships, and work the twelve-steps with a mentor or sponsor. The steps are designed to change the way someone thinks internally as well as how they behave externally. Many recovering addicts whom I know personally as well as professionally utilized and continue to utilize this way of life, incorporating the twelve steps into all they do, allowing them to live in a state of enlightenment while moving them away from probable death.

Just knowing the twelve steps is not enough. Remember, knowledge is not enough. An addict must apply the knowledge for transformation to continue. Each step has a corresponding principle that is the state of mind, behavior, attitude, and belief one should have when they are processing a specific step. It is the virtue needed to pass each step.

The Twelve Steps and Their Corresponding Principles

The Twelve Steps and the principle with each step includes (I have chosen to leave a blank in step 1 because I believe these steps are a way of life and can be used for any addiction. Leaving a blank allows anyone to put whatever they need to in the blank they want to transform. A heroin addict would begin by putting heroin in the blank, but as he or she evolves, anything that a person is powerless over can be worked through using the steps):

1. **Honesty:** I admitted I was powerless over _____ that my life had become unmanageable.

2. **Hope:** I came to believe that a power greater than myself could restore my sanity.

3. **Faith:** I made a decision to turn my will and my love over to the care of God as I understand him.

4. **Courage:** I made a searching and fearless inventory of myself.

5. **Integrity:** I admitted to God, to myself, and to another human being the exact nature of my wrongs.

6. **Willingness:** I am entirely ready to have God remove all these defects of character.

7. **Humility:** I humbly asked Him to remove all of our shortcomings.

8. **Love:** I made a list of all persons I had harmed, and I am willing to make amends to them all.

9. **Justice:** I made direct amends to such people wherever possible, except when to do so would injure me or others.

10. **Perseverance:** I continue to take personal inventory, and when I am wrong, I promptly admit it.

11. **Spirituality:** I sought through prayer and meditation to improve my conscious contact with God, as I understand him, praying only for knowledge of his will for me and the power to carry that out.

12. **Service:** Having a spiritual awakening as a result of these steps, I try to carry this message to alcoholics, and to practice these principles in all my affairs.

The Principles Explained

For anyone to take the first step and admit they are powerless requires an enormous amount of courage and major *Honesty*. We as humans are so good at rationalizations and justifications and making up excuses to act in ways we know are not good for ourselves or the people around us. Addicts usually have so much guilt and shame, the thought of actually admitting that they had no control is very difficult to admit. I believe guilt is a useful feeling, but shame is directly connected to the dark and is used to continue to keep an addict sick and suffering. Guilt means that you feel bad about something you've done. It is a compass that lets us know if we are walking in alignment with our souls. To feel guilty means we need to alter some choices we are making, without judgement and without self-hate. On the other hand, shame means you feel bad about who you are. The light would never want you to feel bad about who you are because it knows this is part of your path, and there is more than meets in the eye and so much we do not know about the human world.

First of all, I have never met a person in actual recovery from opioid, cocaine, crystal meth, alcohol, benzodiazepine, weed, alcohol (fill in the blank) addiction who did not project true light and love. This was not always the case with these individuals. Moving from a lifestyle from the dark into the light is a journey that involves many horrifying behaviors that must not be judged because the journey is not complete. There is so little information or data out there that explains how a beautiful and innocent individual can so quickly turn into a monster fueling darkness and destruction. Remember, in order to know the light, one must have been intimate with the dark.

Hope is believing in things not yet revealed. The key word is believe. Believing that something bigger can restore a sick and suffering addict to sanity. This sounds so out there, but do not knock it until you have seen it. One of the most amazing teachers I have ever met was a recovering heroin addict. He spoke to addicts in a way I had never seen or heard before. I called him the addict whisperer. I believe his life path took him down a road of extreme addiction, only to heal him so he could help heal other addicts. Not only was this individual an example of *Hope*, but he also gave heroin addicts *Faith*, as a walking testimony that a higher power exists, and actually can heal you.

Faith is a hard one. To be willing to let go and allow something else to take over is not just faith, it is blind faith. The idea of not knowing where this new lifestyle is going to take an individual and if this new dimension is going to work for them are all scary thoughts that keep people sick in fear. Many clients have said to me how they would have faith if the Universe gave them a sign to have it. It does not work like this. Start with faith and the signs come.

Courage and *Integrity* are required to release and uncover secrets that have been holding addicts hostage. Having the courage to expose your issues and then being honest when admitting your issues to another person is life changing. It releases energetic strongholds designed to oppress and marginalize, making addicts think they are worse than the next addict. Let me explain something, no one's issues are any better or any worse than another's. Addicts need to stop thinking they are so special, believing that what they have done is worse than the next addicts. You are not that special when it comes to your issues because we all have issues!

I have never done heroin. I have done my share of drugs, but never heroin. I ask clients all the time, "If I want to learn how to use heroin, who would I go to teach me?" They unanimously always say, "A heroin addict." They are correct. I then challenge the heroin addict and say, "then why won't you allow yourselves to be taught by people who have learned to live life on life's terms and have successfully moved from the darkness into the light?" If an addict wants to transform their soul, they have to be *Willing* and *Humble*. They cannot be what they do not know. They have to be willing to be a student, open to learning from people who have transformed from the dark into the light.

Love, *Justice*, and *Perseverance*. These principles go beyond what is required from your normal, everyday individual. They bring people to a level of being that is above and beyond our human state of mind. They allow us to love in an enlightened state, raising energetic vibrations while creating global energetic shifts. To love people enough that we admit who we have harmed and then make amends to these people is so difficult, that many addicts give up at this point. Taking the time to reflect daily on one's choices, decisions, and attitudes requires a level of emotional intelligence needed for this process. Living in this way requires one to live their best life now. The honesty required of this kind of self-reflection must be as brutal as possible for the process to create transformation.

Spirituality meditating on energies that are above the human level of understanding, connecting to a source that continues to guide and reveal hope and love while increasing faith has the potential to bring addicts back to their true selves while utilizing their eagle eyes (we'll talk about this in Chapter 7). It brings them to a place of empowerment instead of victimization. Finally, it allows them to live from a spiritual level of consciousness creating a life that is beyond one's wildest dreams.

Lastly, the spiritual way is not only to receive, but it is also about giving back. It is this beautiful symbiotic relationship of *Service* that is necessary for all spiritual beings. The main purpose of this path is two-fold, learn to live your best life possible while teaching others to do the same and spread the light as only a soldier of the light can.

> *A strong man cannot help a weaker unless the weaker is willing to be helped, and even then the weak man must become strong of himself; he must, by his own efforts, develop the strength which he admires in another.*
>
> — James *Allen, As a Man Thinketh*

This chapter focused on the history of addiction treatment and the incredibly powerful negative stigmas attached to them. It also explains how addicted individuals stepped up and created systems designed to help individuals struggling with addiction embrace their true selves while providing a purpose to give back to other sick and suffering addicts. The next chapter begins the explanation of why the addictive path is so powerful.

Chapter 5:

The Herd or Not the Herd?

SO WHY CAN'T AN ADDICT EVER BE NORMAL? Why can't addicts remain in the human level of consciousness? In this chapter, I will discuss the wonderful opportunity addicts are blessed with. This is not an easy road, but one that is earned. To do the work of the light, one must be ready and prepared. They must not be part of the herd!

So what do I mean by the herd? According to Merriam-Webster, "a herd is typically a large group of animals of one kind kept together under human control; a congregation of gregarious wild animals; a group of people usually having a common bond; a large assemblage of like things." In the treatment rooms, we refer to the herd as normies. One of the first lessons I teach addicts is you will never be a normie (or part of the herd), so stop trying! This is extremely difficult to accept.

Imagine being a young twenty something and being told "you can't drink, or you could die," "you can't smoke weed or you could die," "you can't do a line of cocaine or you could die." Let's be honest, many Americans know when enough is enough. They experience the college life and do their share of mind altering substances that could probably kill an elephant. But many know when enough is enough. A true addict never really knows when enough is enough. A "normal" person or a normies would eventually graduate, get a job, get married, and maybe even have a kid or two joining the reciprocal monotony of the herd living a life of work, home, and sleep, only to get up to do it over again. An addict may follow this pattern on the surface but unfortunately there would probably be a secret life ensuing hidden from those who no longer partake in excessive partying. Addicts cannot be like the "normal" people mentioned above. They cannot join normies at a bar to balance out the stress of the day with a cocktail during happy hour. Their happy hour would turn into an all-night event, missing work or going to work feeling so horrible promising to never party again, only to repeat the pattern the next night. In reality, I really don't know what a normie is, but when it comes to someone who is truly addicted, their life is not meant to be normal. Let me explain.

Enlightened◄—— 👤👤👤👤👤👤👤👤👤 ——►Die

You see, Percocet, Vicodin, Oxycontin, Dilaudid, Adderall, Xanax, Ativan, Klonopin, alcohol, (fill in the blank) are extremely powerful substance that take over the mind, body, and soul when abused. They are so powerful individuals addicted to these substances are willing to give up everything to use them. Yes, everything! I'm talking husbands, wives, children, families, education, careers, homes, cars, youth, health, dignity, God, love, joy, peace, hope, laughter, I could go on. This is hard for non-addicts to comprehend, but it is far bigger of an issue than just the substance alone, and it is definitely not a moral issue as many believed in the past.

Normies, if you will, have options. They have a choice to choose multiple paths. They have a choice to stop the partying and study for the test or write the paper. Choice is the key element in differentiating normies from addicts. An active addict does not have a choice. The choice is taken from them as they are literally possessed by the substance (we will get more into this later).

Normies can live in the grey. The grey is the dimension in the in-between. The in-between is the ability to live a life that involves settling with mediocre feelings of internal joy and peace, not too happy but not too sad, not living a righteous life but not living an unrighteous life. Most of the herd has the ability to live in guilt and shame, sadness and depression, isolation and loneliness, but it's not extreme. It is an acceptance of the reciprocal monotony of life mentioned above. It is in the middle, the grey. Normies do not have to find the strength within themselves to detach from all that exists in this world, while finding peace and contentment in hope, gratitude, love, and forgiveness. I am not saying normies do not have the same opportunity to grow in these enlightened ways, they do, but it is not necessarily life or death.

An untrained addict or an active addict is unable to live in the grey. Their emotions are extreme, and they are highly sensitive to energies. When they feel, they feel hard. Not to mention, the depths of darkness a soul has to travel to in order to continue a lifestyle that is riddled with prostitution, burglary, sexual and physical trauma, extreme physical and emotional pain, and death. Living a reciprocal monotonous life is not a choice for an untrained active addict.

Working with thousands of opioid addicts throughout my career, I noticed most of them were very sensitive as children. Most of them were sensitive to energies and emotions as children that only intensified as they grew into adulthood. In addition, most have powerful energies themselves that project much farther out than a normie's energy. Have you ever heard the saying, "you can cut the tension with a knife"? Well, how is this possible? How does one know when they are feeling tension in a room with other people? You can't see it. You can't touch it, taste it, or smell it, but many people can feel it. Raise that feeling by 100 percent and this is how an addict feels the energy; and once received, this is what they project out. When they love, they love hard. When they hate, they hate hard. When they are angry, it's an all-out black-out rage. When they are in an environment that is hostile or extreme, they will feel it. Extreme! There is no grey as it is very black and white. Unfortunately, the only two options a heroin addict has in this life is to either become enlightened to these truths and adjust their internal and external lives accordingly, or they will die. They must learn who and what they really are within this world, or suppress the truth that their purpose is way bigger than they can even fathom.

Gift or Curse?

For a seed to achieve its greatest expression, it must come completely undone. The shell cracks, its insides come out and everything changes. To someone who doesn't understand growth, it would look like complete destruction.

— Cynthia Occelli

I love this quote! It kind of puts everything into perspective for me and all of the people I've been honored to work for and with. There is not one addict I have met in my almost two decades of doing this work that I have not absolutely adored and seen such amazing potential. They are tasked with striving to be the best "me" they can be. They are tasked with having to address their emotions in a healthy way that creates positive change because if they do not, they will die. It is with great sadness, that I have to report many have died.

"For a seed to achieve its greatest expression it must come completely undone." Let us take a closer look at this. Pain is the great equalizer. A personality trait I have noticed with most of the clients who initially enter treatment is that they are extremely stubborn and prideful. The idea of surrendering to the recovery process is bullshit and many believe they know what they need to get sober. In this altered reality, the only thing left is their own will, and many actually fight to the death to keep it.

In the conflict resolution world, the cessation of drug and alcohol use required to enter treatment no longer allows the addict to avoid the intrapersonal and interpersonal conflicts associated with the lifestyle. This in itself creates intrapersonal conflicts due to the duality of what the individual wants to do versus what they believe they are capable of doing. Addicts will literally manipulate themselves into believing "I am right, and the world is wrong" to justify their desire to get high. The interruption of use alters the conflict style; whereby, avoiding conflict is no longer an option. It is now about competing with others as well as their own spiritual selves to be right. The negative feelings associated with the individual wanting to get high, provides the fuel to create rationalizations and justifications that "I am right, and you are wrong," while having no regard for other people's feelings or positions. What is needed for an addict to change is a shift in their own internal perspective thereby shifting their reality.

The beginning of transformation and enlightenment happens when an individual accepts that their attitudes and behaviors are no longer working for them. This is not easy to accept. This spiritual task can only be accomplished by a soul who already has what it takes inside of them to accomplish it. It just needs to come out. This is when the shell cracks and the reality of where one's life is or is going becomes real. This is extremely painful but is the beginning of absolute transformation of being. The difference between a normie and an addict, this shell cracking must happen for an addict to survive and thrive, or they will die. A former opiate addict explains:

> Pain has a funny way of making you do something you have never done before. Pain has a way of making you want to change. Then there's that type of pain that words can't explain, that not changing isn't an option. If I saw it was definitely going to eventually get better, I wouldn't have surrendered the way I did. I couldn't have taken any more hits. I had no more fight in me, not enough strength to even try to swing back. I was defeated, cold, dark, empty, and near dead. That being said, I believe that pain is a great teacher. Not to say that it is welcomed in any way, but I know when I learn the lesson pain is trying to teach me, my life changes for the better. Conversely, if I don't learn the lesson, there is always more pain. So is being an addict a gift or a curse? Hmmmm, the jury is still out.

JOB 5:7 *but human beings are born to trouble, just as sparks fly upward. Challenges are inevitable.*

Victim Identity

Okay, you really want to know a very important step when it comes to learning a universal lesson? Task number one: Stop being a victim. Merriam-Webster defines victim as "one that is acted on and usually adversely affected by a force or agent. One that is injured, destroyed, or sacrificed under any of various conditions. One that is subjected to oppression or a sense of being weighed down in body or mind."

One of the many problems that comes with addiction is the fact that using mind-altering substances narrows one's perspective, not allowing eagle eyes, or even human and spiritual levels of consciousness to evolve. The ability to tap into these spiritual superpowers remains dormant, but not quiet, as they call to the addict from within, reminding them there is more. In addition, whatever the narrowing perspectives is, it will be extreme.

Many active addicts believe they are addicts because life has been cruel to them. They stay active addicts because of the negative beliefs they have about themselves and the world. They are professional manipulators creating an altered reality aimed at justifying and rationalizing their addictive behaviors to make their lives somewhat bearable. This releases personal responsibility onto the world. Their identity continues to be fed by other addicts who they believe are like them. Negative + Negative = Death!

Having a victim identity as an addict is severely dangerous. Severe is not even a severe enough word to make this point! This belief prevents solution focused thinking due to an altered mental state that suspends positive spiritual growth and exacerbates negative spiritual growth. It is a well-known spiritual fact, in my reality, that there is no such thing as stagnation. Time never stops, which means, one is either moving forward in life or moving backward in life. I have had many clients throughout my career tell me, Nicole, I'm stagnate. I basically tell them they are full of it because if they are not progressing to the light, they are progressing to the dark.

There are infinite amounts of seeds that we as humans have the power to plant within ourselves and for each other. So the seed we are referring to does not necessarily have to be a seed of joy and harmony. Seeds could also be seeds of anger and disharmony. A seed of victimization is a very dangerous seed for an addict. In Psychology Today, Andrea Mathews, LCC, NCC explains it well. The belief systems of the person with a victim identity fall along these lines:

- Life is really, really hard
- Don't get up, you'll just get kicked back down again
- Beware, always beware of trickery; it's around every corner
- You can't trust anyone
- I can't
- You just don't understand how hard it is for me.
- Everyone is always picking on me
- "They" are always bigger, badder, and smarter than me

Multiply the seven characteristics above by 100 percent and imagine living in this world, with this attitude, and believing that it is all true. Sounds like purgatory.

Nancy Carbone for YourTango.com lists ten warning signs to determine if you might have a victim mentality which was printed in an April 2019 psychcentral.org blog. They include:

1. **You Do Not Take Action or You Give Up:** Manipulating your own internal system with rationalizations and justifications to continue with the addictive lifestyle.

2. **You Lack Self-Confidence and Self-Belief:** Lack belief in your own abilities. When an addict does not believe they are anything more than an addict, changing one's lifestyle will be impossible.

3. **You Let Others Take Control Over Your Life:** Giving over your personal power to others. This could be in the form of co-dependency or hanging

on to past memories of people who have wronged you, while holding onto resentments.

4. **You Let Negative Self-Beliefs Sabotage Your Choices in Life:** You give up based on your own negative self-dialogue. You settle for things in life because you may believe you are not worthy of more or will not be able to get more.

5. **You Deplete Yourself Until You Need Support:** Living an active addict lifestyle is extremely difficult. Surviving on the streets, being homeless, eating from garbage cans or not eating at all is exhausting. Closing one's eyes to the many opportunities that present themselves throughout this time eventually brings addicts to a state of desperation. Not taking responsibility for this desperation and projecting blame onto the world keeps people sick and holds them back from learning the lessons.

6. **You Feel Bitter and Resentful That You're Not Living Your Life:** Feeling bitter and resentful keeps people in an energetic realm of self-pity and self-loathing. Knowing in your soul that there is more to life than shooting heroin is both a gift and a curse. A gift because the idea of being more is genuinely felt, but a curse because many do not know how to get out.

7. **You Make Excuses for Why You Give Up:** Self-sabotage is a very real thing. The idea of trying but failing is an extremely powerful fear. Not trying at all means technically, one has not failed because they have not tried. Fortunately, the soul will continue to torment an individual who is destined for greatness, and this torment will hopefully, eventually outweigh the fear.

8. **You Engage in Self-Destructive Coping Behavior:** Coping is the key word here. Utilizing negative coping skills becomes the norm. Avoiding all uncomfortable situations with mind altering substances and negative behaviors becomes reflexive and programed in the brain. Feeling feelings for an addict is going against the very grain of their addict being.

9. **You Beat Yourself Up or Self-Punish:** There is no greater punisher for an addict than themselves. The self-hatred they have puts them in a place where they believe they do not deserve to be happy. If anything remotely good happens to them, they will sabotage it due to the fact they do not believe they are worthy.

10. **It Is Always Someone Else's Fault:** Working in the field of addiction, I have been blamed for clients' misery, relapses, family problems, lack of money, anger, failures, and so on. The victim mentality believes that negative situations are someone else's fault. All the bad stuff going on is a result of other people and no fault of my own. I am failing because of something outside of myself.

The ten warning signs above are very normal thought patterns for active addicts. If an addict believes that they can change their life, then they become responsible. Once there are no more excuses to maintain the lifestyle, it will be more difficult to live in it. Mateo Sol, a prominent psychospiritual counselor and mentor wrote in his article titled; "23 Signs You're Suffering from a Victim Mentality":

> Victim mentality is a psychological term that refers to a type of dysfunctional mindset which seeks to feel persecuted in order to gain attention or avoid self-responsibility. People who struggle with the victim mentality are convinced that life is not only beyond their control, but it is out to deliberately hurt them. This belief results in constant blame, finger-pointing, and pity parties that are fueled by pessimism, fear, and anger.

It was Descartes who coined the phrase "I think therefore I am." The problem with active addicts is that many choose to stay rooted within a victim mentality. It takes responsibility off of them and puts it out into the world. "I'm like this because of _____" fill in the blank. There is no healing in this way of thinking. Victims think they will forever remain active addicts;

therefore, many struggle to alter their victim identity. Many have admitted they belief they are ultimately going to die taking fifty pills a day or with a needle in their arm. This has nothing to do with being weak or not having the ability to change one's mindset. I believe it's really due to fear as Mateo suggests in his writing and the continued negative mindset of the self and the world.

This chapter focused on the difference between a normie and an addict and the disturbing and exciting idea that an addict has two choices in life, they either become enlightened or they die. It talked about the purpose of pain and how with every great movement forward in this thing called life, there will probably be some suffering involved. It talks about the need to break through a victim's mentality and what this mentality looks like.

Fear is also discussed as an energy. Energy attracts energy. If a person suffering with addiction continues to surround themselves with like-minded people who believe they are victims as well, while putting themselves in environments which are infested with this vibration, the seed will come undone, its insides will come out, and the fruit of fear and victimization will swell and nurture a victim identity. If they do not become enlightened to the fact that they could change their victim mentality to one of an empowering/ surviving mentality, there will be no healing.

What are some of the possible reasons people turn to addiction as a coping mechanism? Chapter 6 will attempt to explain possible causes as to why this may happen. The two theories described are just small pieces within a very large puzzle to explain this phenomenon. The goal is to gain some understanding because the more we know our enemy, the more we know how to fight it!

Chapter 6:

How did This Happen?

WITH EVERY YIN THERE IS A YANG. "I think therefor I am." What if an active addict could change the way they think of themselves. What if hope could replace hopelessness and something within is ignited that motivates one to explore possibilities of an altered life? There must come a time when one acknowledges the pain and actually reflects on where it came from. This must occur for the transformational process to begin. But again, this is a choice and the idea of possibilities is very scary for most people. Choice means that we have the power to change our circumstances and to change our energetic vibrations. We can change what it is we are connecting with to from a human and an energetic perspective. This would mean one would need to step outside of their comfort zone and take a risk. The risk includes one of success or one of failure. Possibilities in life mean that there are options. But what if I try and I fail? What if I try and succeed?

There are many people who allow themselves to experience continued suffering because they may believe change is not possible or the fear of making these changes is just too overwhelming. Maybe they hope it will change on its own? Maybe they hope other people will change? Maybe they think if they repress or suppress the pain long enough, it will just disappear? Avoidance will get you nowhere.

One of the powerful functions of opioids is to numb pain. Not only does it block pain messages transmitted through the spinal cord, but it also mutates normal activity in the limbic system which is the section of the brain that controls instincts, mood, and basic emotions like anger, fear, and pleasure, as well as our drives which are hunger, sex, and arousal, just to name a few. Imagine a young fourteen- or fifteen-year-old having access to a mind-altering substance that would cease the need to feel the growing pains of teenage life and keep you in a constant state of Euphoria? (Unfortunately, this is how it traps people to eventually take their souls. We will discuss this in more detail later.)

Imagine all of the profound skills we have the potential to learn as adolescents and teenagers: problem-solving, communication, anger management, conflict resolution, assertiveness, forming friendships, adaptation, love, the pain of love, foundations for our religious or spiritual beliefs, confidence, courage, moving past fear, eating, dressing, moral codes of the groups we identify with as well as our own personal ethics. I could go on! To live life on life's terms is a powerful skill that is learned from birth all the way to our passing on. There are few adult human beings born in this country that have been excluded from the trials and tribulations of the elementary school and high school experience. Throw in a dysfunctional family (which is unfortunately part of this thing called life) and there you have it. A cornucopia of training systems preparing you for the most stressful challenges life will throw your way as you grow into adulthood. But the way we move through these challenges will be our demies or our rise. As mentioned above, there is purpose in pain.

But what if, you never learned the lessons that came with adolescence or young adult pain because you learned how to numb the pain with a pill, a drink, a snort, a smoke, or an injection?

The world has changed significantly since I was a teenager (and I'm not that old). We had pagers and it was the start of AOL. Cell phones were not available and there was no social media. Information was limited. Peer pressure to look a certain way and act a certain way was limited to your peer and social network, and the channels you had on your television were also limited because there was no Xfinity, Netflix, Amazon, Hulu – you get the point.

We are living in a time that allows one to be susceptible to all kinds of dangerous ideals of what one's life should be in order to be deemed successful. With modern internet and social media technologies leading the way in creating a culture that perpetuates an instant gratification mindset, it should come as no surprise that many Americans chose quick fixes to alleviate physical, mental, or social dysfunctions. But it is not working! People are looking in the wrong direction to fill that annoying void we all feel in the depths of our soul. In the infamous words of Paramanhansa Yogananda, no amount of external good fortune will bring lasting happiness and the more you depend upon conditions outside yourself for happiness, the less happiness you will experience. Addicts have very limited choices when it comes to choosing their path. They will either have to learn this or they will die!

Proverbs 20:5 The purposes of the human mind are like deep water, but the intelligent will draw them out.

This is not for the faint or the weak. Going inside the soul and remembering who you really are means going against every grain of your being. It means touching the parts within the self that most people do not dare enter. It is about taking unfiltered passion that involved razor sharp focus, exploiting its power to obtain the drug of choice at whatever cost, creating a life of insanity, and turning it around utilizing the same razor sharp focus to obtain all that comes with a recovery lifestyle, creating a life of sanity for you and those around you. We will get into this much more in depth later. For now, all one needs is a small spark of hope, a mustard seed, and a possibility.

> *Once the soul awakens, the search begins and you can never go back. From then on, you are inflamed with a special longing that will never again let you linger in the lowlands of complacency and partial fulfillment. The eternal makes you urgent. You are loath to let compromise or the threat of danger hold you back from striving toward the summit of fulfillment.*
>
> — John O'Donohue

Let's first take a look at where our initial perspectives may have come from through the lens of two theories I developed based on my years of work learning and teaching Onion Theory and Bubbles Theory. We will start with the Onion Theory.

Onion Theory

What if we never had to leave our mother's womb? Imagine if we could stay there and our mother continued to provide everything for us from her body? I know, sounds kind of weird and boring if you ask me. So why are we born? In the simplest of terms, we are born into this world to forget who we are through our experiences in this thing called life, and then we are called to find our way back. Back to where? This the ultimate question. Many are called but few are chosen. So how do we lose ourselves? What happens to make us forget? And how do we find our way back?

One of the keys for transformation to begin is self-awareness. To begin this process, it will be imperative to understand the transcendent truth that addicts are not just addicts. They are so much more. People do not just wake up and say they want to be an addict! Life experiences move people on a path that creates layers of protection, creating a thick energetic force field around our souls. Unfortunately, these layers become so thick, we actually forget who we really are. Let us take a closer look at this.

1. When we are first born; when we first come out of our mother's bellies, we are the closest to our truest selves then we are ever going to be. Life has not yet manipulated us. Experiences have not shaped us. It is as if you went from one dimension (a 98-degree warm belly needing nothing but a host and a feeding tube) to the next (an external cold world where all levels of communication and human rules need to be learned) with no concept of anything. It is no wonder why babies cry and scream. They are confused and know nothing of this new world.

2. Humans literally start receiving messages and training of what is expected of them in this world from the very second they enter it. These messages move us away from our truest selves creating layers of protection so we fit in to what we think is right, or defy what is deemed normal because of painful experiences. It begins when we are infants. If you are a girl, you usually get put in colors like pink and are gifted with toys like dolls. I googled top gifts for girls ages two through four and a build a flower garden bouquet set was front and center as well as other pink and lavender pretty things. Very "gender appropriate!" If you are a boy, you usually get put in colors like blue and are gifted with toy cars or rough and tough military figurines. Sure enough, I googled top gifts for boys age two through four and trucks and toy remote control play vehicles were listed as the top gifts for this age group.

Before an individual knows who they are, society is instructing them about what they should like or not like, what is culturally and gender appropriate and what is not. Do not get me wrong, I believe us as humans need rules to guide us while providing moral codes. But what if what you are being taught does not align with your soul? For example, my mother would buy me dolls, and I would cut their hair and rip off their arms. I would have much rather played with my brother's race cars and trucks, and I did. I never wore dresses growing up, and I hated the color pink. Why did society expect me to wear a dress? I was nowhere near a girly girl and enjoyed playing soccer, tetherball, and kickball with the boys (and I was actually pretty good at it!). I was not interested in doing what the girls were doing. I wanted to run, get dirty, and kick things. Sadly this was not normal where I grew up, and I was severely bullied by my female peers which broke my heart.

Life may be a bit more challenging for individuals who struggle with conforming to the norms of what society wants. Another common trait that I have noticed among addicts is that they are non-conformists. Most have struggled with the ideologies of cultural norms and are very creative, wanting to just be accepted for just being themselves. As mentioned previously, many addicts I have worked with are very sensitive to energies and reported being emotionally sensitive as children. This is difficult to emotionally and cognitively understand as an adult, let alone a child. The confusion I would hear from the clients I served when they spoke about their adolescents was, why couldn't I just be me and why did people treat me like crap? Why didn't I fit in? What's wrong with me? Why am I so awkward? Their inability to be themselves as a child created layers of defense mechanisms taking them further away from who they really were.

These thoughts have a high probability of creating feelings of inferiority causing a whirl wind of negative emotions about the self. Throw in a perfectionist mindset, which many addicts have, and you have the perfect storm for the seeds of addiction to take root. (Genetic predispositions as well as environmental and familial high-risk factors are also variables that have the potential to plant seeds of addiction, but we will not get into these areas as these are other viable theories that explain much more about this phenomenon and will be included in another book.)

3. As a result of being bullied, feeling rejected, family discord, feeling like an outcast, as well as being sensitive to the negative energies my peers were projecting, coupled with the inability to cognitively understand why this was happening at such a young age, I personally chose the defense mechanism of anger. This was a very thick layer I placed around my heart for protection. I didn't want to feel hurt, so I learned at a very young age to channel feelings of hurt into feelings of anger. The purpose of my anger was to keep people away from me. Protection, but this too had consequences!

4. Being an angry person can be quite lonely and has the potential to create impulsive behaviors that could bring about violence, trauma, and abandonment. Pair this with social media, which compels individuals to compare one's own reality to the (let's be real) fake virtual reality of other's (which normally inadequately depicts one of near utopia) and we are talking about a scenario that has the potential to

be extremely lethal. Intrapersonal and interpersonal conflicts create an "us" versus "them" attitude. Believing that people do not like you, do not understand you, and want to hurt you while it seems like their lives are going perfectly and your life is awful, creates a reality of complete disconnect to the world. The layers become so thick, extending so far out from one's true self, it's no wonder people become lost.

Now imagine a young person who believes they do not belong in this dimension. Now imagine finding other people your own age who have been through similar experiences and have similar personalities and attitudes. To find other individuals who share your pain is very powerful. It brings about connection and fulfills the basic need of belonging. The thought is, if I cannot belong to this group, then I will align with that group. The theory is, because the individual is lost to self, void of identity, they chose to fit in with the group they feel most aligned with based off their perceived self, not their true self. If I do not fit in with the normies (non-addicts), let me fit in with the addicts. This is an incredibly persuasive formula with all of the ingredients to create a very dangerous idea of the self. I think therefore I am, I think like an addict, so I am an addict, and I am now part of the addict group.

Here is the thing with group identification. Without getting too psychologically and sociologically jargon driven, it is very powerful in shaping one's own identity. A quintessential source of identity stems from an individual's perception of a particular social group that they believe they belong to or are a part of. These connections are so powerful that the individual may even lose sight of who they really are before they are aware of being influenced by the group. This includes taking on the group's values and beliefs, even if the individual does not agree with them. This need promotes social categorization which is a primitive social process that includes defining oneself by identifying with the group they believe they belong to.

I have had many clients who shared with me how they started their addiction with Percocet prescribed from an injury. Many would tell me, "I told myself I would never use heroin." They then were introduced to others within their new group who taught them ways of obtaining a better high. This "better high" was short lived, and the need for an even better high became urgent. The answer was heroin. The idea of doctor shopping for the amount of prescriptions needed to sustain the needed high became overwhelming, and this new group taught where to get heroin, which is ultimately cheaper and does not require a prescription. According to my clients, it usually started out with either sniffing or smoking the substance, but this usually led to intravenous use. Fentanyl and Carfentanil are the new generation of street opiates, which supersede the potency of heroin quite significantly and has killed more clients in the past two-years of my career than what other drugs have done in my almost two-decade career put together.

Social theorists believe the group an individual associates with will take on the characteristics of the group thereby creating an identity of the self, based on their groups' characteristics. Criminal activity, family discord, loss of meaningful friendships, unemployment, dropping out of school, and becoming institutionalized and homeless are common life consequences of a heroin addict which exacerbate negative feelings of the self and perpetuate negative behaviors. Even today, heroin use is heavily de-moralized by our society regardless of the full-fledged opioid epidemic we are experiencing and the millions of people who are addicted. This sadly results in negative social and personal stigmas that only bolster stigmatization, marginalization, and continued use. The identities acquired by people suffering with addiction in which their addictive behaviors are a major part of their self-concept presents core identity and even deeper soul issues they will have to face, or they will die.

I've treated many addicts who shared with me that they knew they were not living their best life. They shared how they believed they had a greater purpose but did not know how to access this. This creates an interesting phenomenon. What if an individual discovers, or becomes aware that they are not acting in alignment with their true soul? What if they wake up one day and start to believe their thinking and attitudes are creating behaviors they no longer want to align with? This happened to me. I literally fought a girl for no reason, and I felt so bad I started shaking. There was a time when my anger served me, but then there was other times when it did not, and my soul let me know.

One of two things happens when you wake up to the idea that we are not acting in alignment with your soul: you will continue to live in the same way and your life will continue to self-destruct, or you will make the decision you cannot continue and your life may actually improve. Once an addict decides they can no longer live the way they were living, they will never be able to go back, and the transformational battle begins.

Once the soul awakens, the search begins and you can never go back.

— John O'Donohue

I love the word awakens. It is exceptionally powerful. I believe that if you are not doing what you are supposed to be doing, what is in your soul to be doing, you will feel restless. You will feel like something is wrong. Unhappy, angry, sad, off – you will feel a different kind of pain. Your soul knows when it is sleeping. The problem is that we cover up the truth with so many layers of crap that we cannot see it, feel it, or hear it. Opiates are an extraordinary resource to cover pain, both physical and emotional. But there is extraordinarily more involved with this mind-altering substance than just covering pain.

So far we have learned through the Onion Theory that we are born closest to our true selves before experience shapes us. We create defense mechanisms to protect ourselves from the challenges of life as a way to survive our environments. We feel separated from the norm and begin to identify with groups who we feel are more like "us" and everyone else becomes a "them." The individual will then begin to act in ways that align with the group's core beliefs even when we may not agree with them. We learn from our groups and create our own identities based off the group we believe we belong to. Hopefully, one day we wake up to the idea that we are not acting in alignment with our true soul and this is when the transformational process of becoming who we really are begins.

PROVERBS 19:27 *Cease straying my child, from the words of knowledge, in order that you may hear instruction.*

Bubble Theory

I'm not in this world to live up to your expectations and you're not in this world to live up to mine.

— Bruce Lee

From the time we come out of our mother's belly, we are continuously being trained by our teachers, learning rules throughout our lives that govern our thoughts, attitudes, beliefs, and behaviors. This is inevitable. As children, we do not really have a choice to choose who will be in our lives and who will not. We cannot choose our parents, siblings, actual teachers in school, or even our peers who share classrooms with us. We cannot change where we live or our socioeconomic status. We do not even have the cognitive abilities to process most of the messages we are receiving from a higher perspective because most children have not tapped into these mental/spiritual mindsets. Before we can think on our own, our teachers are thinking for us, creating what they hope will be our belief system. Don Miguel Ruiz in his book *The Four Agreements* calls this a form of domestication. Merriam-Webster defines domesticated as "adapted over time from a wild or natural state to life in close association with and to the benefits of humans. Brought to the level of ordinary people." But what is ordinary? If every culture has their own rules and each generation changes those rules to correspond to its own evolution, whose rules or what rules do we follow? Which is right and which is wrong? So how does this begin?

In the Onion Theory, I talked about literally going from one dimension, being inside our mother's belly, to being transported to a new dimension, into this world. We will call this new dimension Earth. Let us take a closer look at this. When entering the Earth's dimension, we have this beautiful bubble of the self which is an absolute sponge, ready to absorb all the information and stimuli provided. There are very specific macro rules earthlings need to live by but there are also micro rules which are specific laws that govern cultural systems, family systems, religious systems, socioeconomic systems, gender systems, and so on. This is a process which takes years to develop. So who are the initial teachers that govern these rules?

It begins with the self. The self is then introduced to parents, so then all three bubbles overlap, the self, the mother, and father. If there are siblings involved, another bubble would intersect the self, so now there are four intersecting bubbles. Let's add toys, cartoons, TV shows, and diet. All of these are separate bubbles and all intersect, influencing "the self" in their own ways. Let's keep going.

As we get older our new intersecting bubbles include peers, teachers, music, and social media. Let's go further. More bubbles would include books, art, news, politics, religion, cultural norms, sports, and group affiliations. That's a lot of bubbles, and I am sure all of you out there can add twice if not thrice as many more. To be honest, I believe everything is a teacher! Each teacher is in a bubble. The teacher is the information, or the teachings, surrounded by an energy bubble that we pull from based off of what we have come to believe through the process of learning from our initial teachers. Every one of these bubbles intersects with the self, having their own specific influences on the creation of our reality. Let us take this even deeper.

There is an infinite amount of information and energy in social media. There are positive teachings, negative teachings, and everything in between within this forum. There are teachings that preach external beauty being the catalyst for internal peace as well as teachings that promote the power of acceptance and love of the internal self. Platforms that teach love, hate, peace, war and everything in between. The teachings within the social media world are too large for me to grasp. This is the purpose of the bubble. The bubble surrounding the teachings is the filter. It filters out what does not serve our current beliefs which have been developing since we entered the Earth dimension. Utilizing our current belief systems based off our previous bubbles or teachers, information is constantly being filtered creating a slightly altered perspective through each teacher. This process never stops because we are constantly receiving stimuli from the outside world. This is how we create our realities, receiving the teachings we want to receive from the teacher, utilizing the bubble to filter out what we do not want to receive from the teacher or what we are not ready to receive.

It really is mind blowing when one stops and thinks of just how powerful we really are. As mentioned previously, normies do not have to alter their perspective. They may not be happy, they may not be living their best life, but it is not necessarily life or death for them to keep their current lifestyle. It is different for an addict. If their filter filters out or blocks out messages of opportunity, motivation, or hope, they will die. An addict must change their filter if they want to change their life. They must change the filter they used during active addiction. They must believe their lives can change. This internal belief may need to be ignited by external stimuli. For an addict to transform their soul, they must change their bubbles; thereby changing their filters. Notice I do not say change our teachers. I believe teachers are everywhere and are in everything. It is how we filter the information coming from the teacher that produces a reaction or outcome.

PROVERBS 12:1 *Whomever loves discipline loves knowledge, but whoever hates correction is stupid.*

This is not an easy task. Let us think about a newborn baby. They come into this world knowing nothing. They can cry, sleep, poop, and eat. But they learn quickly. It does not take long for a baby to learn that when they cry, mommy or daddy will come running. Soon they learn how to communicate with strange noises. Then they learn how to crawl and then walk. It is not much longer until they learn how to have full-fledged conversations. Teachers are everywhere teaching babies how to do these things. There comes a time during our development when we learn how to block teachings if we do not want to receive them and seek teachings when we do. I call this selective learning. We actually become empowered to choose what we want to learn, and the lessons we want to receive from our experiences.

This is very important when it comes to the rebirth of an individual looking to transform from an active addict to an addict in recovery. Understanding the very high possibility that in the beginning of this process, the addict in training is going to want to cry and it will be extremely uncomfortable in this new world. They must learn how to walk, talk, feel, communicate, dress, and eat, and so on. Throughout this learning experience, the individual must be very careful with the teachers they allow into their lives and how they are filtering information. It is truly about learning all new rules in an entirely new way. To transform from a state of active addiction to a state of true recovery, one must unlearn everything that they have learned and clean out old filters. The goal is not to forget past lessons, but to no longer apply the old lessons learned which do not serve the current or new lifestyle.

In this chapter, we focused heavily on two theories whose ideologies tap into the power of social learning. The Onion Theory believes an addict may begin life happily and peacefully, closest to themselves than they are ever going to be. Unfortunately life experiences teach us, hurt us, and create pain, which inevitably causes us to create defense mechanisms for the purpose of self-protection. These defense mechanisms create layers designed as a tactic to protect ourselves. Sadly, our behaviors then become controlled by our moods. This in turn may guide people to act in ways that are not in alignment with their true soul. Because we are more intelligent then we give ourselves credit for, chances are, we will internally recognize when something is off. Our soul recognizes when we are not acting in accordance with our true selves, and as a result, we get sick. The more we ignore this awareness, the sicker we become. This is the perfect storm for addictions to manifest. As mentioned previously, opioids are one of the best resources for numbing pain, not just physical pain but emotional pain as well.

The Bubble Theory really focuses on who our teachers were and are and how these teachers eventually helped to shape a reality that governs our perspectives about ourselves and the world. Once the foundation of self is created, filters develop that govern what we receive from messages that are inundated with infinites amount of information. We absorb what we believe and ignore what we do not believe. Unfortunately for an addict, this could be very dangerous if one identifies as a victim or has accepted the idea that they are going to die popping pills or with a needle in their arm. The idea of this theory is change your filter, and you will change your perspective. By changing your perspective, replacing the company you keep, revising the music you listen to, blocking social media glamorizing external idols, and altering the places you go, you will eventually change you! The next chapter focuses on the power of perspectives and the idea that regardless of habits and old patterns of being, we can change not only our perspectives, but transform our souls.

Chapter 7:

The Transformational Power of Perspective

SINCE I WAS A LITTLE GIRL, I have always had a cat. I love cats! Jessie is my best friend who has been in my life for the past four years. She was a rescue from a PetSmart, and I adopted her when she was about six months old. Jessie has always been an indoor cat. Her world has been my home, traveling from room to room throughout the day, making herself comfortable everywhere. She loves to look out the window, but I never knew if she realized outside was an entirely new world, or if she just thought the scenery was a very large painting that had moving pictures in it. One day, I decided to open the sliding door and see what she would do (I was right next to her, ready to grab her if she ran). She was petrified and did not go outside or anywhere near the door. I did it again the next day and this time she went towards the door and began sniffing the air. By the third time, she stepped outside very slowly. The curiosity I saw in her eyes was really cool. Jessie literally stepped into an entirely new dimension. She stepped into a world that was always there, but she was never exposed to. New colors, smells, creatures, textures, sounds, and energies surrounded her for the first time. Her world opened like it never had before. Her perspective changed.

There are so many wonderful worlds out there that many of us have never explored. Most addicts have been trapped in their own dark dimension keeping them enslaved in their own personal hells on earth. What if they had the capacity to change their world? Move from one dimension to another. Move from a place of darkness into a place of the light. What if I said that this is not only possible but can be accomplished with a shift in perspective?

The Eagle Perspective

According to Birdsandblooms.com in their article "7 Cool Facts About Bald Eagles, "the bald eagle has been the national symbol of the United States since 1782 and was chosen for its awesome appearance and representation of *freedom* and *strength*. The article also reports that when it comes to sight, eagles have two centers of focus. This gives them "the ability to see forward and to the side at the same time." Their vision is beyond epic. Finally, according to the article, their speed is brilliant while on the hunt for prey, diving up to 100 miles per hour, and in regular flight, they can glide at about 30 miles per hour.

In the article "Native American Eagle Mythology," the first paragraph of the article explains, "Among the Pueblo tribes, eagles are considered one of the six directional guardians, associated with the upward direction, spirituality, and balance....In other legends, Eagles serve as a messenger between humans and the Creator. The golden eagle, also known as the "war eagle," is particularly associated with warriors and courage in battle, and it is golden eagle feathers that were earned by Plains Indian men as war honors and worn in their feather headdresses."

So why would I be talking about eagles in a book that is about addiction? Throughout this book, I discuss the unavoidable reality that if an addict does not become enlightened they will die. The idea of who our teachers were and are, how we shape our perspectives, and how we create life filters are deep thoughts to ponder, but the ability to change and awaken is what this awareness is all about. It was Kristi Bowman in an article titled "11

Signs You May Be Experiencing a Spiritual Awakening," who shared her belief that when we awaken to our truth, we realize we are free. But which truth? The truth of accepting an addictive lifestyle filled with pain and sorrow or the truth of believing life can be full of love and possibilities? The scary but exciting part of all this, it is totally up to the individual. The gift of choice is incredibly powerful and the perspectives one chooses to follow will either move them closer to darkness or closer to the light.

I believe that eagles are one of the most amazing animals on earth, not true, I think all animals are amazing. But when it comes to sight, vision, strength, and speed, this beautiful bird definitely warrants respect and attention. Human beings in general have the ability to view their life through multiple lenses, either viewing it from a high perspective, low perspective, or anything in between. Addicts who want to change their lives do not have the option of viewing their lives from a limited and narrow perspective, which I call the animal perspective. The ability to have two centers of focus and to recognize when our creator is speaking to us are superpowers within our own right that addicts must tap into to transform their souls. The third eye if you will, or the eagle eyes, must be opened to unlock hidden messages within the world specifically and strategically placed by our creator for us to see. These messages are nearly impossible to see with our human eyes only. Let me explain.

Could you imagine trying to maneuver your way through a labyrinth walking on the ground using only human eyes? Holy free holies! How many brick walls would you hit throughout your journey? Would you give up? Would you accept the fact that you are "stuck" in a place with no hope of escaping? Living the life of an addict has a very keen way of bringing people to a state of hopelessness while feeling trapped. Brick walls may appear all around, suffocating and dark with no opening in sight. The blinders covering alternative paths have the potential to manipulate perspectives crushing the possibilities of various life options only creating a dark emotional state that perpetuates continued use. This is where despair and death appear all around.

I have had many clients who were resistant to taking their blinders off or even attempted to see things from a different perspective. The thought of trying to change their lives and failing enabled so much fear that they were not willing to take and were resistant to any suggestions. I ask two things of my clients when I first meet them, but these two things are very difficult. You must be willing to answer the questions, and you must take suggestions. To be willing to answer questions and to take suggestions does not seem all that difficult, but for an addict who has lived a very specific lifestyle, usually a lifestyle focused on getting high or inebriated, this is asking them to go against every fiber of their being. Many clients I work with enter treatment and literally selectively forget the usually horrifying circumstances that pushed them to a place of surrender that brought them to me. One minute they were on the streets sniffing pills and the next moment are sitting in my office answering intimate questions asked by a total stranger. For some, this puts the idea of a possible higher power into perspective. Many have said, "I don't know how I got here." Many have attested to the fact that they should be dead, and they do not know how they are still alive. Stories upon stories of near-death experiences, some actually dying, only to be revived.

PROVERBS 3:5 *Trust in the Lord with all your heart and lean not on your own understanding*

Many addicts I have come across have shared with me and I quote, "Nicole, I know what I have to do, I just have to do it." This is complete and utter poppycock! If most of the clients knew what they needed to do to get sober, I believe they would have done it. The idea of not using is not enough. After putting down the pills and the drugs, addicts are still extremely sick within their bodies, mind, and souls. There is so much more to this than meets the eye. The Universe would not have introduced them to the darkest of places within this world and kept them alive if there was not a specific purpose for this. The idea of just having a purpose brings hope and this is the catalyst needed to ignite the flame to open the mind, waking up the eagle eyes.

One of the most beautiful things to witness is an addict waking up. Waking up means they are finally ready to admit they have no idea what is going on, who they are, and have no idea how to get sober. Opening their spiritual eyes to that which their human eyes cannot see. This is what I call Eagle eyes.

> EPHESIANS 5:14 *For anything that becomes visible is light. Therefore it says, "Awake, O sleeper, and arise from the dead, and Christ will shine on you."*

> 1 PETER 1:13 *Therefore, preparing your minds for action, and being sober-minded, set your hope fully on the grace that will be brought to you at the revelation of Jesus Christ.*

> *"A kind of light spread out from her. And everything changed color. And the world opened out. And a day was good to awaken to. And there were no limits to anything. And the people of the world were good and handsome. And I was not afraid anymore."*
>
> — John Steinbeck, *East of Eden*

The scriptures and quote above say it better than I ever could, but what better way to open one's eyes than to utilize one of the best eyes in nature for spiritual help, the eagle's eyes. Getting though the labyrinth of life when there has been so many walls and obstacles is nearly impossible for most people struggling with addiction. It requires another set of eyes. You see the eagle has the power to look down at the labyrinth as it flies high above viewing the labyrinth's paths from a different perspective. Having this perspective allows the eagle to see the bigger picture, viewing the beginning, end, and everything in between. There are no brick walls blocking the path because all experiences come with a purpose and a lesson, and the debilitating pain which once was a barrier can be avoided due to the ability to rise above them. The awakening awareness that pain and challenges are training mechanisms for growth begins to emerge. The loss of old friendships and relationships bring new opportunities for new fellowships and group affiliations. The experience of being intimate with the dark provides wonderful opportunities to know and become intimate with the light. Shifting perspectives from human eyes to eagle eyes opens doors to new dimensions within this Earth realm and removes brick walls. This will hopefully open a new truth that embraces the idea that we are spiritual beings having a human experience and not the other way around. When an addict grasps this concept, the enigmatic reality of their purpose is revealed! We will talk more about this later.

The Three Levels of Self

Eagle eyes is a shifting of consciousness from a narrow-minded reality to a reality filled with hope and possibilities. Eagle eyes see life from a perspective that believes, no matter what has happened or is happening, there is a knowing that good can come from it! The fact that we as human beings actually have access to multiple levels of consciousness may seem a bit weird, but I can assure you we do.

I cannot think of a better group of people who would understand this concept than drug addicts or addicts in general. They have been exposed to the idea of alternate realities since the moment they put a mind-altering substance inside of them. I believe all mind-altering drugs actually provides a *synthetic* mindfully meditative and spiritual experience. In an article written in Healthline.com, Matthew Thorpe (2017, July 5) discusses science-based benefits of mediation. They include but are not limited to reducing stress, releasing anxiety, generating kindness, enhancing self-awareness, controlling pain, and decreasing blood pressure. When mind altering substances are ingested, smoked, sniffed, or injected, time no longer exists giving one the ability to fully immerse themselves in the moment. Stress is immediately gone, and it is in these moments that anxiety disappears, there is no pain, and blood pressure decreases. In addition, one's mood is better because they are in a euphoric state, generating a kindness that is short lived. I call this a *synthetic* spiritual experience because it is fake, and not created by internal means but by external means, relying on an external resource to accomplish the desired feeling. In reality, when the substance is no longer creating the euphoric effect it turns quickly, manifesting a hell on earth, making the mind-altering substance one's god. An active heroin, cocaine, crack, crystal meth, benzo, alcohol, etc. addict has one purpose, to get more of the desired stuff.

The reality of one's experiences are mutated when high. It is unclear if minutes or hours have passed. Food and water become irrelevant. Our natural human basic needs no longer matter as food is no longer necessary and thirst is minimal, leaving many addicts highly malnourished and dehydrated. An addict's need to belong, be respected, or self-actualize are no longer a priority when under the influence. This level of consciousness or dimension is very dangerous to sustain for long periods of time as our human bodies and minds require specific conditions to survive. However, this state of being is only experienced during the peak of the high, once the individual begins to come down, there is yet another altered state of consciousness and this is the first level of self which I will call, the animal.

I call this level of consciousness animal because it parallels the behaviors of a starving lion and what they would do for food. If a starving lion sees a baby antelope at a watering hole with his herd lovingly gathered a few feet away from it, do you think the lion is going to care if it rips the baby antelope to pieces and eats it? Do you think it will care that the herd may grieve the loss of their young one? Do you think it will care that it is going to affect the entire system of the herd? Absolutely not, and this is the same with an active drug addict who is in withdrawal, craving the drug so badly that it calls to them loudly, taunting and stealing their every thought while taking the gift of choice away.

Many clients who I have worked with have told stories of things they did or had to do to get their next fix. There was no emotion, no conscious, and no remorse at the time. I've had clients rape and be raped, kill other living beings and almost be killed themselves, were stabbed, shot, stabbed and shot others, and stole from innocent strangers as well as from loving family members. I have had clients enter neighborhoods they never would have entered had they not been meeting their dealers. Lying and manipulating in ways that put to shame the best of the best car salesman is normal. Clients who come from good homes but preferred to live on the streets or in trap houses just so they could get their next fix exist in this reality. I've had clients who have had life threatening abscesses on different parts of their bodies but did not care, leaving treatment against medical advice because they so badly wanted to get high.

I call this animal consciousness because there is no reasoning, no logic, no human understanding for the behaviors exhibited. Rules that apply in the human dimension do not apply in the animal dimension. It is truly a place where one kills or they will be killed. It would be impossible to understand this mindset unless you recognized the power of making something your god, your reason for existence, which is what most illicit and many pharmacological drugs eventually do. It brings people to a place where they will literally give up everything, and I mean everything, for their next high. It is like that hungry lion who believes if they do not eat, they will die and nothing is going to stop it from killing the baby antelope, NOTHING!

The next level of consciousness is the human level. This is the dimension where I believe normies hover at. Aman Sharma shares an article in psychologydiscussion.net titled "Difference Between Normal and Abnormal Behavior." This article describes normal human behavior as, "The common pattern of [behavior] found among the general majority is...the [behavior] of the normal. Normal people exhibit satisfactory work capacity and earn adequate income. They conform and adjust to their social surrounding[s]. They are capable of establishing satisfying and acceptable relationship[s] with other people and their emotional reactions are basically appropriate to different situations."

Let's look at this a bit closer. Notice the article states, "normal people exhibit satisfactory work capacity" and "earn adequate money." Satisfactory and adequate seem okay but not accomplished. There is no suffering but there is also a lack of consistent pure joy. You are kind of in the middle, the gray if you will. The article reports on normal people having "satisfying and acceptable relationships." There is that word satisfying again. What makes normal human beings normal is that they are okay with just being normal and are able to conform to the norms of society. This is a beautiful thing, but most addicts would struggle with just being adequate. If addicts have the double edged sword of needing to become enlightened, they must tap into the greatness that all humans have and are. Their path requires they reach levels of self that are hidden from most people. Settling is not an option because it does not tap into this greatness.

I know this sounds crazy hearing about the lifestyle that comes with living in the animal dimension, but it is true. The human dimension would seem glorious for those who were in the animal level of consciousness, because at least there is a level of compassion and empathy, or so normal people would think. Please understand, I am not talking about external gains, I am talking about internal growth. Addicts are extreme and most have black and white thinking. Not to say that people struggling with addiction cannot enter the human dimension. Of course they can ,and they will, they just cannot stay there. This cannot be their home base.

Reciprocal monotony is dangerous for a drug addict, and self-actualization is top priority for an addict in recovery. The people an addict aligns with, the places they go, and the things they deem are important will either propel them to the light or the dark. It will move them to animal consciousness or spirit consciousness. Remember, they are energetically and emotionally sensitive, have lived in dark dimensions, are stubborn, perfectionists, have razor sharp focus, and are tasked with learning and becoming the best version of themselves possible, or they will die. The human level of consciousness does not require an individual to live their best life now. The in-between is livable. The in-between for addicts, will almost always bring them back to active use.

1 Peter 2:9 *But you are a chosen people, a royal priesthood, a holy nation, God's special possession, that you may declare the praises of him who called you out of darkness into his wonderful light.*

Your greatest awakening comes, when you are aware about your infinite nature.

— Amit Ray, *Meditation: Insights and Inspirations*

The third level of consciousness is the spirit. It is within this level where one's self-awareness has evolved and the individual has learned discernment, giving them the understanding of when memories, emotions, and fears of the future may be interfering with the direction of life. It is in this level that we become aware we are no longer a victim and have the beautiful gift of choice. This dimension gives us the ability to recognize the experiences which created the layers around us that moved us further away from our true selves. It brings us to a place where we can utilize pain acquired from these experiences to be our greatest teachers, not our worst enemies. We realize the ability to recognize who our teachers were and what they taught us is. In addition, this level brings one to a point of awakening to the truth that previous lessons are no longer serving our new path, bringing forth much needed knowledge to transform the soul. It is eagle eyes.

There are many people who have great knowledge. I have met many addicts who could quote the big book of Alcoholics Anonymous, literally word for word. I have met many addicts who knew the Bible better than pastors I have trained under. They sound like they got their life together! Unfortunately, many of these students were toxic with ego and believed knowledge was the only thing necessary for transformation, never applying the knowledge they attained, only to relapse back into their own personal addictions and hell. For someone to truly be living in the spiritual state of consciousness, they must be more than knowledgeable, they must be wise.

EPHESIANS 5:15-16 *Be very careful, then, how you live—not as unwise but as wise, making the most of every opportunity, because the days are evil.*

PROVERBS 16:16 *How much better to get wisdom than gold, to get insight rather than silver!*

Wisdom is the right use of knowledge.

— Charles Spurgeon

Knowledge comes from learning. Wisdom comes from living.

— Anthony Douglas Williams

Knowledge is information. Wisdom is applied knowledge. So when we say an addict must either become enlightened or will die, this means there will come a time when the addict will have to choose if they are going to apply the knowledge the creator has provided or not. Every, *not some*, every, *not many*, but *every* addict I personally have met has said to me that they believe there is something more out there. Not all believed in God, but they believed in something. The lifestyle is so intense and extreme that it really forces one to have experiences they cannot explain. This is knowledge in itself. Information is everywhere and the universe always provides two doors, one that goes right and one that goes left. I guess we could say free will is both a curse and a gift, depending on what one does with it. To live in the Spirit level of consciousness means that one is living in Wisdom and continues to focus on progress, not perfection.

Wisdom is a process that takes time. It is having the ability to accept where one is right now knowing that they will be in a different mental, spiritual, and physical place tomorrow. We are smarter today than we were yesterday, and we will be smarter tomorrow than we are today! Living in spirit knows that only focusing on the now is wise because decisions made prematurely do not allow us to have all of the information needed to make the best decision. If a decision needs to be made tomorrow, and not today, I should make the decision tomorrow because I will have more data.

There have been many addicts who were confronted with challenges while in treatment that prompted them to focus on their futures with fear. Many left treatment before they completed their training because they believed they needed to take care of other responsibilities or else. They refused to take any suggestions and completely took their wills back believing "I got this." I cannot tell you how many times clients left treatment stating, "I'm not going to pick up" and "I don't even want to get high." Within days, I would receive a call that this person was back in detox, overdosed, or sadly passed away. An individual connected to their spiritual level of consciousness recognizes the unavoidable truth which is; without sobriety, without learning and applying new ways of life and healing, without connecting to the right people, they will die. Nothing else really matters.

> *Awakening is not a thing. It is not a goal, not a concept. It is not something to be attained. It is a metamorphosis. If the caterpillar thinks about the butterfly it is to become, saying 'And then I shall have wings and antennae,' there will never be a butterfly. The caterpillar must accept its own disappearance in its transformation. When the marvelous butterfly takes wing, nothing of the caterpillar remains.*

> — Alejandro Jodorowsky

In this chapter, we focused on perspectives and the idea that regardless of habits and old patterns of being, we can change not only our perspectives, but transform our souls. The ability to see from an eagle eye's vantage point allows one to see the whole picture, not just the limited viewpoint we see directly in front of us with our human eyes. To see the whole picture brings opportunities of alternate life paths that may not have been noticed previously. In addition, three different levels of consciousness were discussed and the fact that we have access to all of them at all times. How we think, our attitudes, what we believe about ourselves and other's in this world, how we behave, who we align with, where we physically go to spend our time, how we act when we are alone will be our gage to determine which level of consciousness we are working from.

Let us go even deeper shall we. How can we be more aware and in control of what level of being we want to be living from? Chapter 8 will explain specific universal energies from both the active addict mind set versus the recovery mindset based off specific principles applied within one's daily life.

Chapter 8:

What Are You Connecting to?

IN CHAPTER 4, WE LEARNED ABOUT THE TWELVE STEPS and the corresponding twelve principles that go with each step. As mentioned previously, with every yin there is a yang. If there is a source bigger than oneself that can restore one to sanity, that means there is also a source bigger than oneself that can restore one to insanity. There are individuals already connected to a power greater than themselves that restored them to insanity. They have been part of this war since they came out of their mother's bellies as the universe has been training and preparing them for their ultimate purpose.

In my years of working in the treatment industry, a question I always ask my students is, "have you ever done the twelve steps before?" Most say no, they have not. Here is where I have to challenge people. If there is light, then there must be dark. If the twelve steps and principles mentioned in Chapter 4 are designed to bring people to the light, we must know there are polarizing steps and principles designed to bring people to the dark. The truth is that all addicts have worked the steps. If they have not worked them in their recovery, then they worked them in their active addiction. Let us take a closer look.

In order to transform one's soul, awareness of what needs to be addressed must happen. This requires a level of raw truth about the self, the situation, and the ability to take responsibility for one's behaviors and actions. Step 1 is all about admitting powerlessness over alcohol and/ or drugs while accepting how unmanageable life has become. This means one must stop being a victim and start becoming honest. So, what's the opposite of honesty? You guessed it, manipulation. Manipulating the self as well as others about the reality of the situation, while placing blame on external circumstances or past experiences is a form of manipulation used by the dark side. An example of manipulation could be an individual believing they will never be able to stop taking pills or they will never be good at anything but being an addict. If manipulation is occurring, a reevaluation of the energy source being connected to needs to be explored.

Step 2 is all about hope. The belief that a higher power can restore one to sanity provides a small speck of light within a dark world. Hoping life really can change, hoping relationships will improve, hoping financial independence can materialize and be sustained, and hoping the mind will be at peace are all mental perspectives hope can provide. The opposite of hope is hopeless. Hiding a pill addiction requiring thirty to forty pills daily has an insane way of putting people in a position of hopelessness due to the hopelessness we feel to be able to put the pills down. Plugging into the dark side makes people believe they cannot put the pills down. It makes them believe they will never re-connect with family and friends. Feeling hopeless means there is no chance for true joy and happiness. Plugging into the light side makes people believe they can!

The ability to have faith in something invisible from the human eyes requires an open mind, allowing oneself to go into the depths of the soul. It is about connecting to the eagle eye and the spirit level of consciousness. Turning one's life and will over to a source beyond our level of understanding is what faith is all about. The dark side would have you believe that this source does not exist, encouraging mistrust in the process. What a hypocrite it is. There is not one active addict I have met that did not give their will over to their addiction and the source that aligns with this lifestyle. Many had no money, no resources, hadn't eaten, many were homeless, and somehow, were able to support a $1000 per day habit. This would be impossible had they not connected and turned their will and lives over to it. If one is able to accomplish their goals aligned with the dark, they *can* accomplish their goals aligned to the light. Which source have you surrendered to?

Step 4 is about facing the things which have been repressed for years which enabled the oppression, allowing the negative energy within the soul to flourish. It takes courage to write down on paper the very things that we originally thought we were going to take to out graves. These secrets if you will must be released to clean the energetic blocks created by guilt, shame, anger, resentment, and well, you know what I mean. Fear of admitting specific things and fear of facing ourselves is exactly what moves an addict closer and closer into their own personal hell. The courage to complete a fearless and moral inventory of oneself will help to free the soul from energetic bondage. The truth will set you free!

Oh boy, if writing one's fearless moral inventory isn't enough, the next step on this spiritual path is to actually tell another human being the exact nature of your wrongs! This requires a level of such integrity. The dark side wants you to be dishonest. Many complete this step and are dishonest. This is not an ala carte disclosure! You cannot disclose only that which you are comfortable with disclosing. Please understand, by doing this, you will stay sick and suffering because the *real* toxic stuff will remain inside you. All must come out so you can be energetically detoxed. If an individual is being dishonest in this step, they are plugged into the dark. One cannot give 50 percent in this transformational process.

Steps 6 and 7 are truly about dying to the self and allowing God to take all of our defects of character. These steps require a willingness and a level of humility to release that which no longer serves the new path. This is an extremely scary part of the journey because this is when one releases their identity and will probably begin going through an intense identity crisis. This is when the rebirth begins, allowing a higher power to recreate your identity utilizing light energy to do so. The dark side will not be so easily swayed and will be reluctant to let go of any individual it formally had on its side. It will not let addicts go without a fight. It will attempt to tap into pride in an attempt to utilize these character defects and shortcomings to keep people hostage within their personal mental prisons. Releasing them puts people in a place of the unknown, in a dark cave if you will. A place where you no longer are what you were, but you do not know where you are going. It is a place where one does not know who they are in the light or in the dark. The willingness to allow oneself to be led by the light while having faith everything is going to turn out wonderfully is not an easy thing to do. The ability to recognize one must die in order to reborn must be realized. Accepting the loss of identity is a must. This is necessary for transformation to occur.

Step 8 requires a level of self-discipline. To sit down and make a list of all people harmed in the addiction requires time, thought, and action. It takes stepping outside of the self-indulgent mental state of the dark and recognizing what was done affected more than just one person, and amends need to be made to clear out the residual guilt and shame lingering within the self. Step 9 takes this even further, from making a list, to actually making amends to all persons who were wronged unless to do so would hurt them in any way. If one is tapped into the dark, this step may seem unimportant. It may seem like been there, done that, we all need to move on and forget it! These are just more justifications and rationalizations to fulfill one's own selfish needs and give into fears of confronting that which must be confronted so one can truly be set free.

Understanding that we are human being means we must understand we are not perfect. Taking a daily inventory so we keep ourselves in check is what Step 10 is all about. Persevering on our new path so we continue to grow in ways that move us closer to enlightenment! This requires one to review one's day and really assess if everything was done to the best of their ability. This is not about condemnation but about continued learning and growing with a compassion that understands it is progress not perfection. The dark side will want people to get lazy and lose the desire to move forward, so they find complacency with where they are. Remember, addicts are not part of the herd and they will either become enlightened or die! Complacency is not an option.

Step 11 is all about connecting and staying connected. Relationships need time, love, communication, and focus to grow. If one wants to connect and build their relationship with their higher power, they must pray, meditate, and spend time with the very thing they are trying to understand and get to know better. Relationships take time and they are alive, growing in ways that require both party's attention. Building your relationship with your higher power enhances spiritual awareness and opens doors which may have not been noticed had the relationship not grown. Learning how higher power communicates and speaks is an extremely important part of this journey. Our answers are everywhere as the universe always presents options and escape routes within situations which may seem hopeless. The dark does not want people to believe this. He thrives on disbelief. Spiritual awareness or disbelief, which energy are you plugging in to?

Finally, having had a spiritual awakening as a result of these steps, try to carry this message. The double-edged sword of going through an addiction which may have started from prescription medications is that it is very easy to blame the pharmaceutical companies. Remaining a victim to this truth is an option as most professionals in the field are quite aware that many doctors do not explain in detail the addictive potentials of these pills or even the lethal consequence of mixing pills with alcohol. So here is where eagles eyes come in; if individuals are not intimate with the dark, they will never have the capacity to be intimate with the light. I know this sounds crazy, but it's the truth; recovering addicts have the potential to be the strongest light workers on this planet! Once the steps are complete, it is time for the spiritually trained soldier to be deployed and carry the message to others, spreading the energy of the light to whomever crosses their path. This is so much bigger than pills, alcohol, heroin, cocaine, amphetamines, etc. This is a spiritual war and both sides are recruiting. Which army will you join?

EPHESIANS 5:8 *For at one time you were darkness, but now you are light in the Lord. Walk as children of light*

1 PETER 2:9 *But you are a chosen race, a royal priesthood, a holy nation, a people for his own possession, that you may proclaim the excellencies of him who called you out of darkness into his marvelous light*

MATTHEW 4:16 *The people dwelling in darkness have seen a great light, and for those dwelling in the region and shadow of death, on them a light has dawned*

Unfortunately, the dark does not let his soldiers go so easily. Remember, active addicts are immersed in the dark, doing the dark one's bidding. We have just learned the thoughts, attitudes and behaviors to determine if you are working in the light or the dark realms and have gained awareness into which master you are serving based off of your mental state and actions. The side we choose to plug into is a choice. However, the dark will vehemently continue trying to tempt his former soldiers to return to his army. Chapter 9 will explain even further the tactics used by the dark to keep us sick and suffering, so we continue doing his bidding.

Chapter 9:

The Dark's Recruitment Process

✠ IT WAS NO GREAT SURPRISE THE DAY I RECEIVED divine information about the spiritual purpose of addiction, and even less of a surprise of how the pharmaceutical pill addiction has erupted into a pandemic, affecting nearly everyone in this great nation in one way or another. What a wonderful and powerful way for the dark to recruit his soldiers. It is the very thing that can take people from a place of hope and joy to death and destruction. The minute the mind-altering substance is ingested, our spiritual energetic force field is penetrated, leaving us exposed to cosmic powers we truly know very little about. Chapter 8 literally explains how our thoughts, attitudes, and behaviors will determine the energetic side we are plugging into. However, the dark, or the F**king Goblin (FG), is not going to let his soldiers go so easily. Remember, most active addicts worked for the FG spreading strife, contention, chaos, conflict, misery, and darkness. When someone decides to put the pills, alcohol, powder and/or pipe down, the dark knows what this means. It means, his soldier is about to turn away from the dark side into the light. This is the bigger purpose of why addicts have to choose a side, or the side will choose them. This is why an addict will either become enlightened or die!

The FG has many tactics he uses to maintain his army but there are nine main tactics that every addict must be aware of. This spiritual war requires all of its light working soldiers to know the enemy and how it attacks.

> 2 CORINTHIANS 10:3-5 *For though we walk in the flesh, we are not waging war according to the flesh. For the weapons of our warfare are not of the flesh but have divine power to destroy strongholds. We destroy arguments and every lofty opinion raised against the knowledge of God, and take every thought captive to obey Christ*

> *You have to expect spiritual warfare whenever you stand up for righteousness or call attention to basic values. It's just a matter of light battling the darkness. But the light wins every time. You can't throw enough darkness on light to put it out.*
>
> — Thomas Kinkade

It Lies to Manipulate You

The dark will literally whisper in your ear sweet nothings. It will tell you how horrible you are. It will tell you the only thing you will ever be good at is being an addict. It will tell you to just accept how you're going to die with pills in your mouth or a needle in your arm. It wants you to think your life is over and you can't live without the only thing that ever made you feel good. It will tell you how people suck, and it is because of them you became an addict. It will manipulate you the same way you manipulate people! It will lie to you the same way you have lied to people! Inspiring you to think there is no solution is what it wants. You must stop, recognize what is speaking to you, and aggressively tell it to go away!

Limits Your Beliefs

The dark will put fears and doubts in your mind about life, your potential, and your purpose. It does not want you to think you have a place in the army of the light as a powerful light worker. It wants to shred you with feelings of guilt and shame, so healing becomes hopeless. The FG wants you to settle with all things in your life, so you stay buried in your own purgatory. This is unacceptable and you must know these thoughts are being manipulated by something bigger than you that wants to keep you insane. Notice immediately when your mind begins to go down this path, and aggressively tell it to go away!

Makes You Question Your Faith

The FG cannot be reasoned with. What must be understood is that it wants you to hate yourself and everything around you. It wants you to stay sick and suffering. It will make you question your faith, so you keep asking "why God?" Why would a loving God put anyone in such a place of misery? If there was a God, he would've saved me or helped me in some way.

First, we must understand we are living in the fallen realm where both dark and light co-exist, and we have free choice to choose which we are going to allow into our sacred space. I would never say this to a child. Children are different. Their choices are much more limited than adults. I am speaking here to adults.

Second, none of us are done with our journeys. If you are reading this book, God has provided a resource to help you identify what needs to change and how to change it, giving you the help you require. The mind must stay open and our spiritual eyes/ eagle eyes must always be on the lookout for the different windows and doors providing opportunities of moving this way or that way. They are all around us!

Promotes Isolation and Detests Unity

I can't tell you how many times I've heard clients say, "I'm different" or "I'm not like them." I've heard comments like, "I just snort pills" or "I don't do heroin or use needles, so I'm not that bad." Stop! First of all, if you are crushing pills and snorting them up your nose, there is a problem. If you are taking more than prescribed because you like the way they make you feel, there is a problem. Non-addicts do not do this. They do not crush pills, nor do they snort pills up their noses. They do not lie about the amount of pills they have consumed, and they do not hide them from loved ones. One of the beliefs that must change for healing to occur is the fact that you are not so different regardless of where you come from, how much money you have, the color of your skin, etc. Again, the stories may be different, but all have been to their own personal hell. The FG wants you to think you're different. It wants you to think that you are a special case and you do not need anyone to help you put the pills down. You keep saying tomorrow, I'll do it tomorrow!

The FG does not want unity amongst people who are genuinely there to help you with love and support. One of the most beautiful things about a fellowship, from an AA community, church, synagogue, temple, or other religious or holy group, is it's about connecting with people who can provide the positive energy and support needed during these challenging times. If you notice your mind going to a place of disunity and it begins to promote the idea that you are different, acknowledge the thought and aggressively tell it to go away!

Stimulates Feelings of Hopelessness

This negative virtue was mentioned in the previous chapter, which is the dark principle of Step 2 in the twelve steps of AA. I believe this is one of the main tactics used by the FG, so I felt it appropriate to speak about it twice. The FG wants his soldiers to feel that an alternative life is not possible. That to be free from the pills or the bottle is not possible. It promotes the belief that people can't change, relationships will never improve, financial independence is not possible, and there will never be peace of mind. This is unacceptable and a flat out lie! Let's keep it simple shall we. Acknowledge the thought and aggressively tell it to go away!

Encourages Negative Behaviors

The FG loves defense mechanisms and denial. What better way to keep people sick than to constantly inspire addicts to believe their behaviors aren't that big of a deal. Creating rationalizations and justifications to continue addictive behaviors seems maddening, but not to the active addict. These defense mechanisms are a clever way to keep people in denial, and it is a mind game played by the dark to keep people in a position that will not allow them to recognize the truth of the situation until, in many cases, it's too late. Utilizing the first principle of honesty must happen so the real truth of the situation is exposed so it can then be crushed.

Despises Empathy and Compassion

The ability to recognize, understand, and relate to another human being is a form of unity. Remember the FG despises unity; hence, he then despises empathy and compassion. Empathy is connecting to another human being's feelings or pain. Compassion takes it a step further and not only feels what the other feels but responds with loving action. An active addict would struggle with these acts of kindness because they are powered by love and light, not hate and dark. An active addict must shut these attributes off because of the destructive behaviors required to sustain an addictive lifestyle. It is through rationalizations and justifications that one can continue behaving in ways that creates intense amounts of guilt and shame, blocking empathy and compassion towards the very people who love them the most.

Feeds the Soul Anger and Hatred

The dark is all about resentments and anger. These emotions are super fuels that gas up the power of the dark. Remember in Return of the Jedi, Darth Vader wanted his son Luke to kill him. He wanted his anger and resentments to push Luke over to the dark side. Well, this is kind of similar. The FG wants you to be angry at yourself, the doctors who prescribed the pain medications to you, and/ or the people who introduced the substances to you. He wants you to be angry at people who hurt you throughout your life and family members for questioning you all the time. He even wants you to be angry at your addiction! He wants you to be angry from the inside out. The dark not only wants you angry, it wants you to hold onto your anger and keep resenting yourself, people, and the world so you project a toxic energy that not only affects you, but effects all those around you.

Endorses a Victim Mentality

Chapter 5 goes in depth about a victim's mentality, but this is another tactic I believe warrants extra exposure. Staying a victim means staying sick. Staying a victim allows for continued drug use due to disempowering your God given gift of choice. If one believes they have no power, then they have no power. If one believes they don't have a choice, then they don't. Being a victim to life's circumstances will not allow an individual to use their circumstances for the greater good. It is crucial that you learn the lesson of what the light teaches: never let nothing be for nothing. As mentioned previously, I whole heartedly believe a person cannot become intimate with the light unless they have been intimate with the dark. Not only have addicts been intimate with the dark, they visited very dark places within their minds that can only be described as hell. These dark places are so dark that death becomes the solution. And I repeat, many active addicts believe they are addicts because life has been cruel to them. They stay active addicts because of the negative beliefs they have about themselves and the world. They are professional manipulators creating an altered reality aimed at justifying and rationalizing their addictive behaviors to make their lives somewhat bearable. This releases personal responsibility onto the world creating a victim mindset. Understanding that many people have suffered tremendous pain and trauma from their past, it is important to not minimize what happened; but, it is equally important to begin changing how one wants to handle the emotional pain brought on by difficult experiences of the past. When you notice a disempowered victim mentality arising in your mind, acknowledge the thought and aggressively tell it to go away!

Know Your Enemy

The FG is a dark muse designed specifically for your destruction and the destruction of those around you. It focuses on instant gratification so it can eliminate ultimate happiness. It uses everything it knows to attack in ways designed specifically to kill you. It utilizes mind altering substances as a way to possess and oppress. It finagled its way into the pharmaceutical industry and uses the professionalism of doctors to do its initiating. The time to choose a side is close, but for addicts, even closer due to the universal doors and connections that have been opened as a result of the addiction. So how do we prepare to fight this war? Chapter 10 explains how you are the general of your army and what is needed to win this spiritual battle.

EPHESIANS 6:12 *For we do not wrestle against flesh and blood, but against the rulers, against the authorities, against the cosmic powers over this present darkness, against the spiritual forces of evil in the heavenly places.*

Chapter 10:

The Warrior Within

EPH. 6:11-17 *Put on the full armor of God, so that you can take your stand against the devil's schemes. For our struggle is not against flesh and blood, but against the rulers, against the authorities, against the powers of this dark world and against the spiritual forces of evil in the heavenly realms. Therefore put on the full armor of God, so that when the day of evil comes, you may be able to stand your ground, and after you have done everything, to stand. Stand firm then, with the belt of truth buckled around your waist, with the breastplate of righteousness in place, and with your feet fitted with the readiness that comes from the gospel of peace. In addition to all this, take up the shield of faith, with which you can extinguish all the flaming arrows of the evil one. Take the helmet of salvation and the sword of the Spirit, which is the word of God.*

IT IS IN THE SPIRITUAL LEVEL OF CONSCIOUSNESS that one recognizes they are the general of their army. If a country was going to war with another country, what kind of soldiers would you want to be fighting for you? Wouldn't you want to trust them and know they had the knowledge and the wisdom to defeat life and death battles? Wouldn't you want the best resources and weapons to fight with confidence and courage, knowing that you had everything you needed to be successful? Wouldn't you want the strongest armor possible protecting you? Wouldn't you want to know your enemy, how it fights, where it is most powerful, and how to weaken it?

Metaphorically speaking, an individual struggling with an active addiction are the two battling countries within one mind. One side of you is the enemy of the other side of you. A fight between the two sides of the self must be fought. These two sides are severely polarized creating such a profound conflict. The only resolution is to choose a side and make no mistake, one side is will-win. Having this information, it is imperative that the individual is prepared both internally and externally. Knowing when it is time to apply knowledge learned from the past to defeat the battles of today requires a keen awareness of appropriate timing. Not all battles need to be fought. Battles must be chosen wisely.

75 Watts of Energy

Think of yourself as a 75-watt lightbulb. These 75 watts are the energy needed to get one through the day. I happen to be a very ritualistic person. When I get up in the morning I make my coffee, watch Joyce Myer on the television, and then the news (only the traffic and weather because I'm not a news girl). I make my lunch, shower, and then off to work. Time is of the essence because being ten minutes early to everything is very important to me. Imagine, if you will, a ritualistic person like me waking up, and I'm out of coffee, the cable is out, and I have to stop for gas when I'm running five minutes later than I would like? This may not seem like a big deal for some, but in terms of energy, my stress level due to my rituals being blocked would deplete about 20 watts of energy well before I stepped into my office.

Now I get on the road and someone cuts me off in the car and I lose it (I lived in New Jersey for fifteen years and picked up some of their cultural emotional responses)! My mind is telling me how this person who cut me off deliberately woke up this morning to piss me off and ruin my morning. I'm thinking of this person the entire way into work, which is about thirty minutes. By the time I actually get to work, I'm down another 20 watts, leaving me at 35 watts by 8:30 a.m. So, I continue to go about my day, meet with clients, and do some individual sessions, crisis intervention work, and a three-hour group on spiritual warfare. By noon, I am completely depleted of my watts, and I still have five more hours and four more clients to see. I'm exhausted, haven't taken a break, and now my spiritual energetic force field is down.

This is the perfect time for the FG to begin whispering sweet nothings into my ear inspiring me to believe I work too hard, these people don't deserve my time, and why do I work for so little money and no recognition? I start to get frustrated and angry which leads to resentments, totally forgetting I am an ambassador for God and am employed to train other light workers struggling in the dark. I'm now at a negative 30 watts, and I still have two clients to see. They pour their hearts out to me and I don't care anymore, I'm sick of hearing people's bull! They feel my negative energy, and one at a time feed into my dark energy and begin to question why they decided to go to treatment. Later that night, both clients leave and relapse, and I just lost two students of the light to the dark. Hopefully they don't overdose.

The above scenario is a hypothetical, but is it? How many times has my negative energy affected the very people I am trying to train? It is very important that we recognize when we are not energetically fit and make sure we do something to replenish and refuel when necessary. In addition, not all battles need to be fought. For example, I could have gotten my coffee at the gas station when I went to fill up gas. I definitely should not have taken it personally when the driver cut me off. I mean really. The driver deliberately woke up that morning to ruin my day? I'm not that important! I also could have re-scheduled my sessions knowing I wasn't in the best frame of mind. No matter how ridged we believe ourselves to be, we must become flexible.

The Bamboo that bends is stronger than the oak that resists

— Japanese Proverb

Notice that the stiffest tree is most easily cracked, while the bamboo or willow survives by bending with the wind

— Bruce Lee

We are a society of people living life with negative watts. For normies, this is not okay but not necessarily life or death. For addicts, walking around with negative watts will kill you. Remember, you will either become enlightened or you will die. Keep in mind, the FG wants you dead and knows the time to attack will be when you are hungry, angry, lonely, and/ or tired. It is not a question of if you are going to be attacked but when. That being said, preparation is necessary. Individuals who have struggled with pill addiction, alcoholism, and/ or addiction in general have been intimate with the dark. They know what it feels like, smells like, tastes like, and looks like. Remember, they were there. It is imperative to become aware when energy levels are low and do what is necessary to rest and refuel the mind, body, and spirit. As the General of your army, you must be ready to go to war whenever war is being waged but taking care of yourself is not enough. You need soldiers!

Your Soldiers

Hand picking and utilizing new positive support networks recruited as your army must be done as wars are not won by single individuals alone. Characteristics to look for in your soldiers should include an indomitable spirit or a person who provides strength and hope regardless of extenuating circumstances. Your soldiers should be life-long learners, never believing they have finished learning what the universe is forever teaching. Your soldiers should be loyal to their higher power and to the cause of the greater good! They must have integrity, be honest, and have strong moral principles. They must be hard workers for their own personal and spiritual growth. They should be encouraging, loving, and servants. They must possess what the general wants. If we are going to fight this war, we must learn and follow godly soldiers. Soldiers are there to protect and support. They will fight with you when you do not feel like fighting anymore. They are the energy needed when your energy is depleted. They are the gas, the strength, and the human connections required to bring us closer to the divine.

Let me remind you, the FG is not going to let his dark soldiers go so easily. The temptations that will arise must be fought in a way that is superhuman. The crazy part, addicts are very familiar with their dark enemies because they were one. What better general could there possibly by then one who actually fought for the other side and knows it personally?

As mentioned previously, this level of spiritual warfare relies on a keen awareness of what the dark looks, smells, acts, sounds, and feels like, which all addicts have mastered. Individuals addicted to pills know this because they have been very intimate with the dark. It counts on divine discernment of what is for you and what is against you. This level of consciousness elevates an individual to a soldier status where they are prepared to do battle with the very energy that does not want them to move forward, utilizing free will and human desires of the flesh as its weapon. This cannot be done alone! This battle is not about one's personal will, human strength, or even desire to get sober. It is much bigger and cannot be fought by fists, guns, knives, angry words, or even a strong desire to stop.

Opioids, the Devil's Candy

Opioids have become the devil's candy. It is the temptation used to lure its victims into his grasp. He makes it to where it starts out seductive, a utopia on earth that cannot be described to anyone who has never experienced this dimension. It is a love affair beyond human comprehension because it takes away all pain, all discomfort, all fears, all doubts, all cares, and all worries.

But something happens. It becomes everything and everything becomes nothing. It brings people to a mental place of which nothing else matters except making sure the *candy* is in your life.

I picture it like the scene in Raiders of the Lost Ark when Indiana Jones and Marian were tied up and the German's stole and opened the Ark of the Covenant (Oh man I'm really giving hints about my age now). Spirits came out of the Ark initially appearing beautiful with white glowing skin and big soft eyes only to transform into a hideous looking skeleton faces screaming death and destruction. All who had their eyes opened and looked at the spiritual beings died a pretty gruesome death. This is the devil's candy, pills that tempt people with beauty and comfort only to take away everything, and I mean everything, leaving people with horrendous skeletons in place of what once was.

The crazier part of all this is most addicts are logically aware of what's happening once the denial disappears, but this logical awareness is not strong enough to tear oneself away from the candy. The dark knows this and after the initial temptation, will utilize its dark tactics mentioned in Chapter 9 to keep people connected to him. The beautiful part of all this is we are stronger, we are more powerful, and the power of choice becomes our superpower when we decide to give our will over to the care of God as we understand him!

This chapter stresses the importance of choosing our battles and the power of choice. We really do have the power to create or destroy depending on what we are focused on and what we are connecting to. Chapter 11 brings more clarity to the power of choice and the importance of understanding the difference between instant gratification and ultimate happiness.

1 COR. 10:13 *No temptation has overtaken you except what is common to mankind. And God is faithful; he will not let you be tempted beyond what you can bear. But when you are tempted, he will also provide a way out so that you can endure it.*

1 PET. 5:8-9 *Be self-controlled and alert. Your enemy the devil prowls around like a roaring lion looking for someone to devour. Resist him, standing firm in the faith.*

Chapter 11:

Many are Called, Few are Chosen

✠ IT TAKES A RESILIENT SOUL TO SURVIVE an active addict lifestyle, not to mention adaptability, focus, mental and emotional strength, and perseverance. These are qualities that should not be dismissed. These are qualities that were learned to make sure there was success in obtaining the drink or drug regardless of the external circumstances. Putting the pills down does not require one changing who they are, but becoming who they are, utilizing many skills learned from the dark world. The twist, they must now be utilized for the light. This means the intention of why the skill is being used and what it's being used for must change. The outcome of what one wants to bring into their sacred space must change as well. This requires one to shift one's entire lens of life as well as rebirth a new pair of glasses.

I cannot stress enough, one cannot live by the same rules during an addictive lifestyle as they would in recovery. Recognizing the idea of unlearning what has been learned from our teachers and experiences is a necessary component of this transformation. However, filtering out the negative energy of memories which we attach to must happen to free the self of that which no longer serves your new path. This is not a small task! Many are called but few are chosen or can actually fulfill this soul transformation without sitting on a mountain in some far-off country for decades pondering the meaning of life with no distractions.

The difficult fact when entering the path of recovery is that immediate pleasure is not going to be obtained. Actually, the opposite is true. It will suck! The rules of the recovery world in terms of communication, hygiene habits, daily living routines, socializing, events, eating, sleeping, etc. is nothing like it was living in the active addict dimension. In the active addict dimension it is all about instant gratification. Feeding the desires of the human body is the priority no matter who gets hurt. Remember, it is in the animal state of consciousness where only reflexes and impulses are present. This active addict world never allows for ultimate happiness because what it desires is not truly what the heart or soul desires. It is what the flesh desires! It will provide instant gratification but it will never provide ultimate happiness. This is how the dark feeds its victims.

In the recovery world, one must learn how to sacrifice immediate pleasure so ultimate happiness can be obtained. Sacrifice is the key here! This includes, sacrificing everything one thinks they want, what the body is telling you it wants, and even what the mind is craving, and believing it cannot live without. Now really consider the power of addiction. This can be seen in the sacrifices made for recovery versus the sacrifices made for the pills or alcohol. Let's take a closer look at this. As mentioned previously, active addicts will give up everything (families, jobs, money, homes, cars, morality, peace, joy) for the pills, but many will not give up the pills for everything (families, jobs, money, homes, cars, morality, peace and joy). This is not logical, rational, and makes no sense whatsoever to people who do not understand its power. Sacrificing immediate pleasure literally will shock a system which has been feeding itself instant gratification for years. There was pain and suffering to sacrifice for the pills and there will need to be pain and suffering to sacrifice for recovery. One must not rush the process!

Many are called but few are chosen does not mean the many who are called do not have what it takes to transform. It means many are not willing to do what it takes to transform and not willing to go through the pain and sacrifices necessary to get there. Let's look at the wonderful story of the three little pigs shall we.

The Three Little Pigs with a Nicole Twist

Once upon a time there were three little pigs. The mamma pig knew it was time for the pigs to leave the home and become big pigs. She hired Mr. Beaver, who was an amazing house builder to come and teach her sons how to build a strong house with a solid foundation that could withstand anything, while providing protection from all pork predators. All three pigs were so excited to start a new life and ran out of their mother's house with only the clothes on their backs (Yes, pigs wear clothes in this story).

The first pig found a beautiful spot in the forest and didn't think he needed to take the suggestions of Mr. Beaver. He wanted his house built quickly so began gathering the easiest material he could find, straw. So in a rush was this pig to make his home, he never planned for any challenges he would face. Within a few hours, he was overjoyed and snickered at the instructions of Mr. Beaver, believing his way was a much better way. He made a beautiful little hut and even made a bed and a chair he could sit in during lazy days.

One day he heard a knock at the door and a mean voice demanding "Little pig, little pig, let me in". The pig ran to his window and saw this horrible big bad wolf and shouted, "not by the hair of my chinny, chin, chin!" The wolf yelled back, "then I'll huff, and puff, and blow your house down." The pig started laughing believing he was safe in his straw home. Within seconds the wolf huffed and puffed blowing the house down. The pig had nowhere to go, and sadly, became breakfast.

Now pig number two heard what happened to his brother and decided he would plan a little better and not make his house out of straw. He was incredibly tired though, and he knew he wanted his house to be made quickly, so he only followed some of the suggestions of Mr. Beaver, believing the small details did not matter. He walked through the forest gathering nearby twigs and made a beautiful little house. He even made a bed and a chair he could sit in during lazy days.

One day he heard a knock at the door and a mean voice demanding, "Little pig, little pig, let me in." The pig ran to his window and saw this horrible big bad wolf and shouted, "not by the hair of my chinny, chin, chin!" The wolf yelled back, "then I'll huff, and puff, and blow your house down." The pig started laughing believing he was safe in his twig home. Within seconds the wolf huffed and puffed blowing the house down. The pig had nowhere to go and sadly, became lunch.

Pig number three heard what happened to his brothers and so badly wanted to live. This need to live life and fulfill his dreams was so powerful he decided he was willing to follow every suggestion Mr. Beaver made to build his home. He walked two miles to the local hardware store and bought everything Mr. Beaver told him to buy. After finding the best location in the forest, little pig number three began building his home. He used a mason line to set the bricks. He used a story pole to guide the bricks. He used a spade trowel to apply the mortar, laying each brick carefully, using the trowel to scrape any excess mortar. He even cut bricks to make smaller bricks for the ends of his walls. After hours upon hours of grueling work, pig number three built himself a solid home with a solid foundation. He did not rush the process and patiently took his time, fighting his urge to rush the process. He even made a bed and a chair he could sit in during lazy days.

One day he heard a knock at the door and a mean voice demanding, "Little pig, little pig let me in." The pig ran to his window and saw this horrible big bad wolf and shouted, "not by the hair of my chinny, chin, chin!" The wolf yelled back, "then I'll huff and puff and blow your house down". The pig did not laugh and prayed with all his might the house he built would withstand the attack! Within seconds the wolf huffed and puffed but nothing was coming down. He huffed and puffed again and again and again. The house didn't move. After one hour of the wolf huffing and puffing he fell over dead due to the loss of oxygen from huffing and puffing. Pig number three went outside, and grabbed the wolf who, gratefully, became dinner. The End.

I hope I did not offend anyone with this story, but the reality is; it takes pain, suffering, and hard work to transform one's soul. You have to be willing, and you have to take suggestions. I have worked with many addicted individuals who cut corners and do what I call a la carte recovery. Picking and choosing what to follow because it's quick and/or feels more comfortable has not only hurt people but destroyed them. Pill addicts believing their addiction is not so bad because it's *only* prescriptions is a lie. Alcoholics thinking alcohol is legal and it's a social thing, so I should be able to do it too like everyone else is a lie. These mind sets manifest a very dangerous position, creating excuses that what must be done doesn't have to be as severe as a heroin addict. To be quite honest, some of the worst withdrawal and post-acute withdrawal symptoms I have seen have come from doctor prescribed pills that individuals became dependent on and very quickly addicted to.

The Dark Cave

If you noticed in the three little pig story, all three pigs were initially very excited to begin their new quest and become adult pigs destined for success. Unfortunately, two out of three were tired and chose not to do what was required for success. This has been the case with many clients I have worked with. They begin motivated, only to lose motivation and turn back to old ways. It's like starting a diet after a big meal when you're not hungry. This is the exciting time of the transformation where hope is alive, but the pain of suffering is not yet experienced. It is what I call the dark cave when we see if the rubber meets the road.

The dark cave is when a person knows they no longer want to be who they were but don't know who they are yet. It is a time of confusion, darkness, and is meant to bring about an identity crisis. This is when the mind starts to battle with itself, one side wanting to go back and the other side wanting to move forward. The people you have around you, the places you go, and the things that are deemed priority will be paramount during this time. This is when the old identity must die so a new identity can be reborn. This new identity is very susceptible to influences so who one has as their teachers and who one has in their scared space is crucial. A grieving process will occur and the need for a positive social support network and fellowship is key to help one move through the stages of grief so acceptance of the loss is obtained.

It is usually during this time when reservations are held onto because the idea of letting go is too painful. Reservations could include old prescriptions, phone numbers of specific doctors, and staying connected to people who are known to be negative influences for this new path. This could include holding on to old belief systems that keep one stuck in a negative or victim mentality. Hanging on to significant or insignificant others who continue to enable or partake in addictive behaviors will make it nearly impossible for an addict fighting for recovery to let go and let God. Have you heard the saying, you can't have two gods? This is it. The dark cave is the time when one must choose a side, chose their teachers, chose their friends, chose their environments, choose what they are willing to do and sacrifice to get where they want to go. For most, the beginning of this process isn't the hard part. Once in the dark cave, the body and the mind will be screaming with grief and loss and will torment the mind by thinking the pain will never leave. But we now know from Chapter 9, this is one of the dark's tactics to keep you sick and suffering: lying! I have worked with many individuals who are no longer in the dark cave and have entered a new world of love, beauty, peace, and joy.

When the student is ready the teacher will come. It may not be in the way we think, but higher power always finds a way if one is willing. This process requires the individual wanting to transform to be a very active participant in the process. One must be open to possibilities and energies of this world that we have very little information about. Finally, you must believe, this too shall pass!

Chapter 12:

The Chosen Ones

✠ I HAVE BEEN ON A QUEST TO FIGURE OUT this thing called addiction since I took my first introduction to drugs and alcohol class in college. Listening to the professor talk about the behaviors and the horrors that went with addiction explained a lot about my first boyfriend and why he treated me the way he did. It also explained why I was the way I was. As I learned more and more about this issue, I began to realize it's a lot bigger than I could have ever imagined. Science can only explain so much.

As a child I believed life would be very different when I became an adult. As a kid there was nothing more important than smiling, laughing, playing with my friends, and enjoying the moment. The excitement of recess, summer vacation, riding my bike, playing in the backyard, eating ice cream, hanging out with my brothers, watching movies, and the ability to just be were easy for me as a child. As my experiences intensified, so did my life. Being exposed to energies I could not explain as a little girl opened my mind to explore things I probably would not have explored. Shutting my mind down as a young teenager from all the internal and external chatter appeared impossible and created a lot of anxiety for me. My life changed drastically when I learned how a mind-altering substance could alter my perspective, creating a temporary internal utopia, moving me from a place of anxiety to a place of peace. It opened a door to another dimension I did not know existed.

The pain of my first alcoholic boyfriend, the pain of my family moving away and leaving me alone with this alcoholic boyfriend, the pain of abuse and trauma, the pain of rejection, abandonment, and grief opened other doors to dimensions creating an adventure I am still involved in. These experiences taught me how taking mind altering substances transports people to alternate dark dimensions where the dark angels just wait for the perfect opportunity to take their soldiers and make them theirs. I learned just how true this spiritual warfare is. However, as a result of my trainings, teachers, higher power, and newly filtered mind, how I respond to the twists and turns of this adventure are very different than before. Looking back, I now know the purpose in the pain, something I was unable to see until recently.

This book is designed to help people understand that when they take mind altering substances, they are in essence disconnecting themselves to the light and utilizing a source bigger than them bringing them to a place of insanity. My hope is that individuals struggling with prescription addictions, alcohol, and illicit substances understand this is not a moral issue, it is an issue of the soul and spirit. Addicts have already tapped into universal energies beyond their level of understanding and in order to fight it, they have to know what they are up against. Knowing the tactics of the dark and how it tries to keep us sick and suffering, using low level energies to fuel us so we continue to spread darkness and despair is the purpose of opioids, benzos, and amphetamines.

Once trapped inside the active addiction dimension, it is very difficult to get out. Identities became polluted due to societal and personal stigmas attached to the idea of addiction and what the world believes it to be. Thoughts about the self and the world are dark and ominous because this is the dimension of active addiction. Climbing out of one's personal hell requires a kick ass soldier that surpasses all levels of human understanding. Knowing who your teachers were, how you came to believe what you believed, and recognizing the fact that you are not living in alignment with your true soul is half the battle. When the student is ready the teacher will come.

The idea that addiction could be a universal training method provided by God to teach his soldiers how to be his best light workers may seem like a farfetched idea, but one I very strongly believe in and have dedicated my life to. Having been intimate with the dark gives recovering addicts an advantage as a soldier of the light. They know what the dark smells like, acts like, looks like, feels like, sounds like, moves like, and how it lies and manipulates. They know it very personally.

It is extremely important for me to help guide addicts into the light and teach them they have a choice of which side they want to fight for. I wrote this book to recruit other light workers. Training up and coming students, ready to learn what the pain was all for makes the pain worth it. Teaching individuals who are ready to serve a new god, ready to join the cause of becoming a light worker, and eventually becoming a recruiter of the light is the enlightened result of this journey. I chose the side of the light and commit to my mission as an ambassador for God, working for him to help recruit others who have been dancing with the devil and don't even know it.

Join me!

Acknowledgments

This book would not have happened had it not been for the love and support of my mother, Laura Toggweiler, who talked me out of many dark times when I wanted to give up. Words cannot express the gratitude I have for what you did for me through this process. You are not only my mother, but you are also my best friend. I love you.

To my wonderful father who was the calming force throughout this process, never feeding off my anxiety while always providing words of encouragement. Watching TV together cleared my mind more than you know. I would like to thank my step-father who has always believed in me. Our intellectual conversations were not only stimulating but also helped me recognize I had knowledge that needed to be shared. I love you both.

To Dr. Angela Lauria, KristaLyn Montrose, and Ramses Rodriguez, big thank you for providing a platform and foundation to help amazing people reach amazing goals.

Finally, thank you to my Lord Jesus Christ. Without Him none of this would have been possible. You have moved mountains in my life to allow this to happen. You are my everything!

About the Author

Nicole Ouzounian received her master's degree in addictions counseling from Fairleigh Dickinson University in Madison, New Jersey, and her PhD in conflict analysis and resolution from NOVA Southeastern University in Davie, Florida. She is a master certified addiction professional with over fifteen years of experience in the addiction field, providing treatment for adults, adolescents, and families in recovery.

While working for the Saint Barnabas Healthcare System in New Jersey, she was recruited for prevention specialist and operational director for the Institute for Prevention. In that role, she managed and facilitated a state-recognized educational program teaching anger management, conflict resolution, nutrition, and drug and alcohol prevention throughout the tristate area.

Relocating to Florida, Dr. Ouzounian focused her career on treatment, becoming responsible for the day-to-day operations of a partial hospitalization program, intensive outpatient program, and faith based program for a privately-owned treatment center in Boynton Beach, Florida. Working in the field of addiction enlightened Nicole to the true strength of the human spirit. She has witnessed and helped individuals transform from despair to discovering their strength and wisdom within themselves. Nicole continues to guide addicts from the dark into the light in South Florida.

Thank You

I want to thank everyone who has supported this book and all the amazingly wonderful addicts I have learned from. Changing the negative stigma of addiction while helping people realize their full potentials of what recovery can manifest has been my life long study and dream. I am here to educate, answer questions, provide support and guidance, as well as listen to any feedback you may have. Please feel free to contact me, Dr. Nicole Ouzounian, at Dr.nicouz@gmail.com to learn more about how you can tap into your truth or help those struggling find their way to a life beyond their wildest dreams.